This book belongs to:

Christmas 2001

Christmas
with **Southern Living**
2001

Christmas
with Southern Living
2001

Edited by Rebecca Brennan,
Julie Gunter, and Lauren Brooks

Oxmoor
House.

©2001 by Oxmoor House, Inc.
Book Division of Southern Progress Corporation
P. O. Box 2463, Birmingham, Alabama 35201

Southern Living® is a federally registered trademark belonging to Southern Living, Inc.

ISBN: 0-8487-2431-3
ISSN: 0747-7791
Printed in the United States of America
First Printing 2001

Editor-in-Chief: Nancy Fitzpatrick Wyatt
Senior Editor, Copy and Homes: Olivia Kindig Wells
Senior Foods Editor: Susan Payne
Art Director: James Boone

Christmas with Southern Living 2001

Editor: Rebecca Brennan
Foods Editor: Julie Gunter
Associate Editor: Lauren Caswell Brooks
Copy Editors: L. Amanda Owens, Cathy Ritter Scholl
Editorial Assistant: Suzanne Powell
Editorial Intern: Marye Binkley Rowell
Associate Art Director: Cynthia R. Cooper
Senior Designer: Emily Albright Parrish
Senior Photographer: Jim Bathie
Senior Photo Stylist: Kay E. Clarke
Stylist Assistant: Cathy Mathews
Illustrator: Kelly Davis
Director, Test Kitchens: Elizabeth Tyler Luckett
Assistant Director, Test Kitchens: Julie Christopher
Recipe Editor: Gayle Hays Sadler
Test Kitchens Staff: Rebecca Mohr Boggan; Jennifer A. Cofield;
Gretchen P. Feldtman, R. D.; David Gallent; Ana Price Kelly; Jan A. Smith
Contributing Test Kitchens Staff: Kathleen Royal Phillips, Kate M. Wheeler, R. D.
Publishing Systems Administrator: Rick Tucker
Director, Production and Distribution: Phillip Lee
Books Production Manager: Larry Hunter
Production Assistant: Faye Porter Bonner

WE'RE HERE FOR YOU!
We at Oxmoor House are dedicated to serving you with reliable
information that expands your imagination and enriches your life.
We welcome your comments and suggestions.
Please write us at:
Oxmoor House, Inc.
Editor, Christmas with Southern Living
2100 Lakeshore Drive
Birmingham, Alabama 35209

To order additional publications, call 1-205-445-6560.

For more books to enrich your life, visit
oxmoorhouse.com

CONTENTS

CHAPTER 1

ENTERTAINING MENUS

Open your home, and invite friends to gather and share some fancy food and good cheer. The following pages are all about holiday parties and how to make them exceptional.

Set the stage for this holiday meal with an antique white theme. Adorn the table with winter white blooms and mix and match ivory china. Light snowball candles, and let their glow beckon you to the feast. For more details, see pages 26-27.

SOUTHERN-STYLE CHRISTMAS DINNER

Southern ingredients shine in this upscale feast. Ham, hash browns, grits, and turnip greens get sophisticated twists in this mouthwatering menu displayed in a dreamy white setting. Southerners love to set a fancy table—see page 26 for tips on the elegant white Christmas decor.

Menu for 8

Gorgonzola Cookies • Cran-Horseradish Sauce and Cream Cheese

Holiday Ham with Cumberland Sauce

Grits Dressing • Crusty Macaroni and Cheese

Mustardy Beans with Buttered Almonds

Sweet Potato Hash Browns • Spicy Turnip Greens

Eggnog Pie • Hazel's Fresh Coconut Cake

Christmas Countdown

Relax and enjoy your own party when you follow this easy-paced plan.

1 week ahead:
- Make grocery list. Shop for nonperishables.

2 or 3 days ahead:
- Get out china, serving dishes, and utensils. Polish silver.
- Shop for perishables.
- Bake Gorgonzola Cookies.
- Prepare Cumberland Sauce. Cover and chill.
- Plan centerpiece. Make place cards.

1 day ahead:
- Prepare Cran-Horseradish Sauce. Cover and chill.
- Brown sausage and prepare grits for dressing. Cover and chill.
- Trim green beans. Cover and chill.
- Cook sweet potatoes. Cover and chill.
- Prepare Eggnog Pie. Cover and chill.
- Bake cake layers. Prepare fresh coconut.

Christmas morning:
- Set the table.
- Prepare and bake Crusty Macaroni and Cheese.
- Prepare Boiled Frosting. Assemble and frost coconut cake.

3 to 4 hours before the meal:
- Bake Holiday Ham.

1 hour before the meal:
- Prepare and serve Cran-Horseradish Sauce and Cream Cheese. Serve Gorgonzola Cookies.
- Finish preparing Grits Dressing and bake.
- Prepare Spicy Turnip Greens.
- Prepare Mustardy Beans with Buttered Almonds.
- Prepare Sweet Potato Hash Browns.

Just before serving:
- Reheat Cumberland Sauce for ham.
- Reheat Crusty Macaroni and Cheese.
- Brew coffee.

GORGONZOLA COOKIES

Serve these savory cookies with your favorite vintage, or stack them in a cellophane sleeve and tie them to a bottle of wine for a hostess gift.

¾ cup walnut pieces, toasted
1 cup all-purpose flour
½ teaspoon salt
½ teaspoon freshly ground pepper
3 tablespoons cold butter, cut into pieces
4 ounces Gorgonzola cheese, crumbled

Process walnuts in a food processor just until ground. Add flour, salt, and pepper; pulse until blended. Add cold butter, and pulse 5 or 6 times or until crumbly. Add crumbled cheese to processor, and process just until a dough forms and begins to leave sides of bowl.

Shape dough into 2 (5") logs. Wrap in wax paper, and chill several hours or until firm. Cut into ¼"-thick slices, and place on ungreased baking sheets. Bake at 350° for 10 to 12 minutes or until lightly browned. Cool 1 minute on baking sheets; remove to wire racks to cool. Store in an airtight container up to 5 days. **Yield:** 2½ dozen.

Gorgonzola Cookies

Cran-Horseradish Sauce
and Cream Cheese

CRAN-HORSERADISH SAUCE AND CREAM CHEESE

This is cranberry sauce to write home about. It gets a surprise pungency from horseradish and a sweet splash of sugar. It's a beautiful jewel-toned appetizer when spooned over cream cheese. Or you may choose to give a gift jar of it to the cook.

1 (16-ounce) can whole-berry cranberry sauce
½ cup sugar
⅓ cup minced onion
2 tablespoons prepared horseradish
½ teaspoon salt
1 (8-ounce) package cream cheese
Garnishes: fresh rosemary sprigs, fresh cranberries

Stir together first 5 ingredients in a medium saucepan. Bring to a boil, stirring often. Remove from heat. Cover and chill 1 hour or up to 3 days.

When ready to serve, spoon Cran-Horseradish Sauce over cream cheese on a plate. Garnish, if desired. Serve with assorted crackers. **Yield:** 8 servings.

Display a smorgasbord of holiday food in white dishes old and new. (Counterclockwise from front) Holiday Ham with Cumberland Sauce, Sweet Potato Hash Browns, Spicy Turnip Greens, Mustardy Beans with Buttered Almonds, Crusty Macaroni and Cheese, and Grits Dressing give family members delicious options.

HOLIDAY HAM WITH CUMBERLAND SAUCE

For a moist, juicy, herb-infused ham, bake it in an oven bag with rosemary sprigs. The sweet, tart English sauce highlights red currant jelly, citrus, and port wine, and spices up each slice of ham.

1   (7- to 10-pound) fully cooked spiral-sliced ham half
     (we tested with Smithfield spiral-sliced Honey Ham)
8   to 10 fresh rosemary sprigs
1   oven cooking bag
Garnishes: fresh rosemary sprigs, fresh cranberries
Cumberland Sauce

Unwrap ham, and remove plastic disk covering bone. Tuck rosemary sprigs randomly between every 2 or 3 slices of ham. Place ham, cut side down, in an oven cooking bag; place in a 13" x 9" baking dish. Close bag with tie. Trim excess plastic to 2". Cut 3 (½") slits in top of bag. Bake at 275° on lowest rack for 2½ hours or until a meat thermometer inserted registers 140°.

Remove ham from oven; let stand in bag with juices 15 minutes. Remove ham from bag, and transfer to a carving board. Separate slices, and arrange on a serving platter. Garnish, if desired. Serve with Cumberland Sauce. **Yield:** 10 servings.

CUMBERLAND SAUCE
1   tablespoon butter or margarine
¼   cup minced onion
1   (12-ounce) jar red currant jelly
1   tablespoon grated orange rind
¼   cup orange juice
1   tablespoon grated lemon rind
¼   cup lemon juice
1   tablespoon Dijon mustard
1   cup port wine

Melt butter in a saucepan over medium heat; add onion, and sauté until tender. Add jelly and next 5 ingredients; cook over medium heat, stirring often, until jelly melts. Add wine; simmer, uncovered, 5 to 10 minutes. Serve warm. Cover and store in refrigerator up to 5 days. **Yield:** 2 cups.

Ham Pointers

• Start with a spiral-sliced ham. It's already baked and sliced. All you do is reheat it. Follow our recipe that yields moist, juicy meat enhanced with rosemary flavor.

• Buy the shank end of the ham; it has a tapered, pointed end. Its bone configuration makes it easier to slice than the butt end.

• Many grocery store spiral-sliced hams come with an enclosed packet of glaze. If yours has a packet, save it for another use.

• After you've baked the ham, juices will have accumulated in the oven cooking bag. Drizzle juices over ham slices once you've arranged them on a serving platter.

1. Unwrap ham, and remove plastic disk covering bone.   *2. Tuck rosemary sprigs between every few slices of ham.*

3. Place ham in cooking bag; close bag with tie and trim plastic.   *4. Cut slits in cooking bag.*

GRITS DRESSING

There's no need for gravy here. This unique Southern dressing stands alone and sports crusty grits croutons and spicy sausage. Make the croutons and brown the sausage a day in advance.

3   (10½-ounce) cans condensed chicken broth, undiluted
1¼ cups uncooked quick-cooking grits (we tested with Quaker)
¾   cup freshly shredded Parmesan cheese
1   pound ground hot pork sausage
5   celery ribs with leaves, finely chopped
4   garlic cloves, minced (about 1 tablespoon)
1   large onion, chopped
⅓   cup butter or margarine, melted
1   large egg, lightly beaten
½   cup chopped fresh parsley

Bring broth to a boil in a large saucepan. Stir in grits, and return to a boil. Cover, reduce heat, and simmer 7 minutes or until grits are thickened, stirring twice. Stir in cheese. Remove from heat.

Spoon grits into a greased 13" x 9" baking dish. Cover and chill until firm. Unmold onto a large cutting board, sliding knife or spatula under grits to loosen them from dish. Cut grits into ¾" cubes. Place in a single layer on a large greased baking sheet or jellyroll pan. Bake at 450° for 20 minutes; turn grits, and bake 10 to 12 more minutes or until crisp and browned.

Meanwhile, cook sausage in a large skillet, stirring until it crumbles and is no longer pink; drain.

Sauté celery, garlic, and onion in butter 5 minutes or until tender. Stir together onion mixture, sausage, and grits croutons, tossing gently. Drizzle egg over mixture; add parsley, stirring gently. Spoon dressing loosely into a greased 11" x 7" baking dish. Bake, uncovered, at 350° for 35 to 45 minutes or until browned. **Yield:** 8 servings.

CRUSTY MACARONI AND CHEESE

A thick, white Cheddar cheese sauce coats macaroni under a crisp topping. Make the whole dish the morning of the feast; then reheat it for 5 to 10 minutes in the oven just before serving.

1   (16-ounce) package large elbow macaroni
½   cup butter or margarine
½   cup all-purpose flour
4   cups milk
4   cups (16 ounces) shredded white Cheddar cheese
2   teaspoons salt
½   teaspoon freshly ground pepper
½   teaspoon hot sauce
3   cups soft breadcrumbs (homemade; see Note below)
6   tablespoons butter or margarine, melted

Cook macaroni just until tender according to package directions. Drain and set aside.

Melt ½ cup butter in a heavy saucepan over low heat; whisk in flour until smooth. Cook 1 minute, whisking constantly. Gradually whisk in milk; cook over medium heat, whisking constantly, until mixture is thickened and bubbly. Add cheese and next 3 ingredients; stir until cheese melts. Stir in macaroni.

Spoon macaroni and cheese into a greased 13" x 9" baking dish or other large baking dish. (Dish will be very full.) Toss breadcrumbs with 6 tablespoons melted butter until crumbs are well coated. Sprinkle over macaroni.

Bake, uncovered, at 350° for 30 minutes or until thoroughly heated and top is golden. **Yield:** 8 to 10 servings.

Note: Make fresh breadcrumbs easily by tearing a few pieces from a French baguette. Pulse bread in a food processor or mini chopper until you get coarse crumbs.

MUSTARDY BEANS WITH BUTTERED ALMONDS

Coarse-grained mustard contributes tang to these beans, and bacon adds that smoky element we all love.

2½ pounds fresh green beans
2   bacon slices, chopped
2   cups water
¼   cup butter or margarine
½   cup slivered almonds
2   tablespoons coarse-grained mustard
1   tablespoon honey
½   teaspoon salt
¼   teaspoon freshly ground pepper

Wash beans; trim stem ends. (Leave beans whole or cut to desired length.)

Cook bacon in a Dutch oven over medium heat until crisp. Add beans and water to bacon with drippings in Dutch oven. Bring to a boil; reduce heat, partially cover, and simmer 12 to 15 minutes or until beans are tender. Drain well, reserving bacon with beans.

Melt butter over medium heat in Dutch oven; add almonds, and sauté until lightly toasted. Stir in mustard and honey. Add beans, bacon, salt, and pepper; toss to coat. **Yield:** 8 servings.

SWEET POTATO HASH BROWNS

Sweet potatoes, honey, and rosemary blend beautifully in this rustic side dish. The key to success is chilling the partially cooked potatoes; this helps them keep their shape in the skillet.

4   large sweet potatoes, peeled and cut into ¾" pieces (3½ pounds)
1½   tablespoons chopped fresh rosemary
¾   teaspoon salt
½   teaspoon pepper
½   medium-size purple onion, chopped
6   tablespoons olive oil, divided
2   teaspoons honey

Cook sweet potato in boiling water to cover 8 minutes or until barely fork tender (not soft); drain well. Spread potato in a single layer in a 13" x 9" pan. Cool; cover and chill at least 8 hours.

Stir together rosemary, salt, and pepper.

Sauté onion in 2 tablespoons hot oil in a large non-stick skillet over medium-high heat until golden. Remove onion to a large bowl.

Increase heat to high. Add 2 more tablespoons oil to skillet, and heat oil until hot. Add half of sweet potato, and sauté 10 minutes or until well browned. Stir in half of rosemary mixture. Add sautéed potato to onion in bowl. Repeat procedure with remaining 2 tablespoons oil, sweet potato, and rosemary mixture; add to potato and onion in bowl, drizzle with honey, and toss gently. Serve immediately. **Yield:** 8 servings.

SPICY TURNIP GREENS

Several convenience products make this recipe appealing, in addition to garlic, Worcestershire, and a hint of lemon. Water chestnuts lend a little crunch.

½   cup finely chopped onion
½   cup finely chopped celery
2   large garlic cloves, minced
2   tablespoons butter or margarine, melted
2   (10-ounce) packages frozen chopped turnip greens
1   (8-ounce) can sliced water chestnuts, drained and chopped
1   (10¾-ounce) can cream of mushroom soup, undiluted
2   teaspoons Worcestershire sauce
¼   teaspoon grated lemon rind
6   to 8 drops of hot sauce
Salt and pepper to taste

Sauté first 3 ingredients in butter in a large saucepan until tender.

Cook turnip greens according to package directions; drain well. Add to saucepan. Stir in water chestnuts and remaining ingredients. Simmer, uncovered, 5 minutes, stirring occasionally. **Yield:** 8 servings.

Eggnog Ethos

*Each year, Southerners celebrate eggnog, the dairy-rich dessert drink, and its ties to
the holiday season. One sip of the silky smooth nog, and it's likely to bring back fond memories
of family recipes and Christmases past. Here's a glance back at the beverage's beginnings.*

History has it that eggnog was brought to the U.S. from Europe, that it was first an English creation, descended from the British drink *posset*, which consisted of eggs, milk, and ale or wine. Eggnog is obviously related to milk and wine punches, such as posset, that originated long ago in the Old World and were often used to toast one's health.

With its European roots and simple ingredients, eggnog fast became a popular wintertime beverage throughout Colonial America. It had much in its favor; it was rich, sweet, and spirited. Once eggnog made it to the New World, the wine was replaced with rum. And in Colonial America, rum was called *grog*, so one can imagine how the term eggnog might have evolved. Here in the South, bourbon promptly became the choice spirit in the holiday beverage.

The recipe for eggnog (eggs beaten with sugar, milk or cream, and spirits) has fared favorably across the states, and its rich flavor transforms all kinds of decadent desserts, such as Eggnog Pie (pictured at right).

Eggnog today remains a popular and socially anticipated sipper at Christmastime. It's hard to imagine a holiday season without an offering of eggnog to warm one's spirits and add merriment to the occasion.

You can enjoy eggnog without the alcohol—just substitute some melted vanilla ice cream and a splash of rum extract.

EGGNOG PIE

We've captured the familiar flavor of eggnog in this silky pie filling and poured it into a cookie crust painted with chocolate.

2   cups pecan shortbread cookie crumbs (we tested with Pecan Sandies)
⅓   cup butter or margarine, melted
½   cup semisweet chocolate morsels
2¼ cups whipping cream
⅓   cup sugar
½   cup bourbon or rum
½   teaspoon freshly grated nutmeg
1   envelope unflavored gelatin
¼   cup cold water
6   egg yolks, lightly beaten
1   tablespoon butter or margarine
Freshly grated nutmeg
Powdered sugar
Unsweetened whipped cream (optional)

Stir together cookie crumbs and ⅓ cup melted butter; press firmly into a greased 9" deep-dish pieplate. Bake at 350° for 8 minutes. Remove crust from oven, and sprinkle chocolate morsels into warm crust. Let stand until morsels melt; spread chocolate over bottom of crust with a spatula. Set aside.

Stir together whipping cream and next 3 ingredients in top of a double boiler; bring water just to a simmer. Cook over simmering water 15 minutes or until sugar dissolves and mixture is thoroughly heated.

Meanwhile, sprinkle gelatin over cold water in a small bowl; let stand 1 minute.

Gradually whisk about one-fourth of warm cream mixture into egg yolks. Add to remaining warm cream, whisking constantly. Whisk in softened gelatin. Cook over hot (not boiling) water 3 to 5 minutes or until gelatin dissolves and custard reaches 160°. Remove from heat; add 1 tablespoon butter, stirring gently until butter melts. Cool filling to room temperature.

Pour filling into prepared crust. Gently cover with plastic wrap, pressing directly on surface of filling. Chill pie at least 4 hours or until firm.

Sprinkle nutmeg and powdered sugar over pie before serving. Serve with dollops of whipped cream and more nutmeg, if desired. **Yield:** 1 (9") pie.

Note: *The chocolate layer will harden after the pie chills in the refrigerator. Use a sharp knife and gentle pressure to slice pie.*

Eggnog Pie

HAZEL'S FRESH COCONUT CAKE

Fresh coconut cake is the very essence of Christmas. Southerner Hazel Burwell has been making this stately cake for her family for over 40 years. She brushes the layers with a fresh coconut syrup to keep the cake moist, and adds marshmallows to the frosting to keep it soft.

1   cup butter, softened
2   cups sugar
4   large eggs
2¾ cups all-purpose flour
2   teaspoons baking powder
1   teaspoon salt
1   cup milk
1½ teaspoons vanilla extract
1½ teaspoons almond extract
2   tablespoons sugar
¼   cup fresh coconut milk
Boiled Frosting
2   to 3 cups fresh shredded coconut

Beat butter at medium speed with an electric mixer until creamy; gradually add 2 cups sugar, beating well. Add eggs, 1 at a time, beating until blended after each addition.

Combine flour, baking powder, and salt; add to butter mixture alternately with milk, beginning and ending with flour mixture. Beat at low speed until blended after each addition. Stir in flavorings. Pour batter into 3 greased and floured 9" round cakepans.

Bake at 350° for 20 to 25 minutes or until a wooden pick inserted in center comes out clean. Cool in pans on wire racks 10 minutes; remove from pans, and cool on wire racks.

Combine 2 tablespoons sugar and coconut milk. Microwave at HIGH 30 seconds; stir until sugar dissolves. Brush 1 cake layer with half of coconut milk mixture, leaving a ½" margin around edges. Spread with 1 cup Boiled Frosting, and sprinkle with ½ cup shredded coconut. Top with second cake layer, and repeat procedure. Top with remaining cake layer. Spread remaining frosting on top and sides of cake; sprinkle with remaining coconut. **Yield:** 1 (3-layer) cake.

Note: *Cover and chill cake for easy slicing.*

BOILED FROSTING

1½ cups sugar
½   cup water
4   egg whites
½   teaspoon cream of tartar
⅛   teaspoon salt
6   large marshmallows, cut into small pieces

Combine sugar and water in a heavy saucepan. Cook over medium heat, stirring constantly, until mixture is clear. Cook, without stirring, until syrup reaches soft ball stage or candy thermometer registers 240°.

While syrup cooks, beat egg whites at low speed with an electric mixer until foamy. Add cream of tartar and salt; beat at medium speed until soft peaks form. Increase to high speed, and add hot syrup in a heavy stream. Add marshmallows, a few pieces at a time. Beat until stiff peaks form and frosting is thick enough to spread. **Yield:** 7 cups.

Hazel's Tips for Cracking Coconut

Here's how to open, clean, and shred fresh coconut. One coconut should yield enough meat and milk for this cake.

Working over a pan or bowl, strike coconut with a hammer several times until coconut cracks in half. Strain coconut milk through a fine sieve, and set milk aside.

Place coconut halves in a heavy-duty zip-top bag; seal. Strike with hammer to get several small pieces. Separate outer shell from meat with a dull knife (an oyster knife works well). Carefully cut away thin brown skin with a paring knife or vegetable peeler.

Rinse coconut meat. Shred coconut in a food processor, using the fine shredder disk. Tightly pack chunks of coconut in food chute and shred, using firm pressure. Otherwise, you can use the largest holes of a box grater to shred coconut—just watch your knuckles.

TABLE TIPS FOR A WHITE CHRISTMAS

Snowy candles, white dinnerware, and pristine blooms set a winter-white table for Yuletide gatherings. Silver flatware and sparkling crystal glasses add glistening accents. These pictures suggest more ways to enhance an all-white theme.

▲ White plates, cups, and serving pieces are a good beginning for an all-white theme. Since place settings compose a large part of the table's surface, using one color is an easy way to achieve a dramatic overall impression. Mix different patterns and pieces for rich texture.

◀ Create an angelic scene for displaying dessert. Cluster wispy paperwhites as the backdrop. Fill in with varying heights of candlesticks and creamy candles, and nestle an angel statue near the desserts.

Individually, these centerpiece arrangements are simple; multiplied by three and lined down the center of the dining table they make an impressive statement. White amaryllis and delicate paperwhites rise majestically from containers filled with clusters of grapes, tiny lady apples, and sliced star fruit. Feathery cedar cuttings soften the edges, and holly and rosemary add fresh fragrance. White egg cups take a turn as votive holders and contribute a warm glow at each place setting. Snowball candles sit atop small weathered garden urns. For place cards, hand-torn paper name tags are tied to the urns with sheer ribbon. ▶

Stand linen napkin rolls in a bowl and stack plates close by so guests can easily serve themselves. Ivory ribbons and pearly buttons add elegance to these easy-to-make napkin holders. Make a set to complement your holiday table, and, while you're at it, make extras to give as hostess gifts. For instructions, see page 166. ▼

Crystal candlesticks, cake stands, cookie and candy jars add light and sparkle to the celebration. The stands and jars become creative serving pieces for the sweets. Velvety roses and gold ribbon embellish beaded trees with bold color. Show off the trees in serving pieces such as an antique silver wine bucket, compote, and tureen.

CANDLELIGHT DESSERT PARTY

Host a sweet soiree this season.
Much of this menu can be made ahead,
so you can enjoy the fun and food
as much as your guests.

Dessert Buffet for 24

Chocolate-Toffee Bars • Cream Cheese Cookies

Brown Sugar Brickle Bars

Fennel Cookies • Holiday Fig Cake

Orange-Pecan Tassies • Rum Fudge Cakes

Chocolate-Peppermint Bundt Cake

Mocha Punch • Coffee

CHOCOLATE-TOFFEE BARS
Each layer of this bar cookie is like a dessert on its own.

½   cup butter or margarine, melted
1¾ cups crushed teddy bear-shaped chocolate graham cracker cookies
1¼ cups almond brickle chips (see Note, opposite page)
6   (1.4-ounce) English toffee candy bars, crushed
1   cup (6 ounces) semisweet chocolate morsels
1   cup chopped pecans
½   cup chopped walnuts
1   (14-ounce) can sweetened condensed milk

Line a 13" x 9" pan with aluminum foil, allowing foil to extend over ends of pan. Pour melted butter into pan. Sprinkle chocolate crumbs in bottom of pan; press firmly, and bake at 325° for 5 minutes.

Layer almond brickle chips and next 4 ingredients over crust in pan. Press layers down firmly. Pour condensed milk evenly over top.

Bake at 325° for 30 minutes or until edges are lightly browned. Cool completely in pan. Lift foil out of pan. Cut into bars. **Yield:** 2 dozen.

CREAM CHEESE COOKIES
Cream cheese and toasted pecans enhance this cookie dough. The result is a delicious alternative to chocolate chip cookies.

¾   cup butter, softened
1   (3-ounce) package cream cheese, softened
¾   cup sugar
¾   cup firmly packed light brown sugar
2   large eggs
2   cups all-purpose flour
2   teaspoons baking powder
1   teaspoon salt
1   teaspoon vanilla extract
1½ cups pecan pieces, toasted
¼   cup cream cheese, softened
2   tablespoons powdered sugar
1½ tablespoons milk

Beat butter and 3 ounces cream cheese at medium speed with an electric mixer until creamy; gradually add sugars, beating until light and fluffy. Add eggs, 1 at a time, beating until blended after each addition.

Combine flour, baking powder, and salt; add to butter mixture, beating well. Stir in vanilla and pecans. Cover and chill 1 hour.

Drop dough by rounded tablespoonfuls 2" apart onto ungreased baking sheets. Bake at 350° for 10 to 12 minutes or until edges are golden. Cool 2 minutes on baking sheets; remove to wire racks to cool.

Beat or whisk together softened cream cheese, powdered sugar, and milk until smooth. Drizzle glaze over cookies. Let stand 1 hour or until set. **Yield:** 3½ dozen.

(Left to right) Chocolate-Toffee Bars,
Cream Cheese Cookies,
Brown Sugar Brickle Bars

BROWN SUGAR BRICKLE BARS

Rich bars, these are. Cut them into small pieces and brew some good coffee to go along.

1   (16-ounce) package light brown sugar
¾   cup butter or margarine
3   large eggs
2½ cups all-purpose flour
2½ teaspoons baking powder
½   teaspoon salt
1   (10-ounce) package almond brickle chips (see Note)
1   cup chopped pecans
2   teaspoons vanilla extract

Cook brown sugar and butter in a saucepan over medium heat until butter melts and mixture is smooth. Remove from heat; cool slightly. Add eggs, 1 at a time, beating after each addition.

Combine flour, baking powder, and salt; add to sugar mixture, stirring well. Stir in brickle chips, pecans, and vanilla.

Pour batter into a greased 13" x 9" pan. Bake at 350° for 30 to 32 minutes. Cool in pan on a wire rack. Cut into bars. **Yield:** 2 dozen.

Note: Find almond brickle chips next to chocolate morsels on the baking aisle.

FENNEL COOKIES

Crushed fennel seeds give these buttery cookies a faint licorice flavor.

1   cup unsalted butter, softened
1   cup sugar
2   large eggs
3   cups all-purpose flour
1   teaspoon baking powder
½   teaspoon salt
2   tablespoons fennel seeds, crushed
1   tablespoon vanilla extract
Sugar or turbinado sugar

Beat butter at medium speed with an electric mixer until creamy; gradually add 1 cup sugar, beating until light and fluffy. Add eggs, 1 at a time, beating until blended after each addition.

Combine flour, baking powder, and salt; add to butter mixture, beating just until blended. Stir in fennel seeds and vanilla.

Divide dough into 2 portions; roll each portion on wax paper into a 12" log. Freeze 2 hours or until firm.

Cut each log into about ¼" thick slices, using a sharp knife; place slices on ungreased baking sheets. Sprinkle cookies with desired sugar. Bake at 350° for 10 to 11 minutes or until edges are barely golden. Cool 1 minute on pans; remove to wire racks to cool. **Yield:** 8 dozen.

Fennel
Cookies

HOLIDAY FIG CAKE

A little chopped fresh rosemary works magic in this moist spice cake. The pecan-studded sides are optional because the cake, once frosted, is snowy white and beautiful.

1¾ cups fig preserves (a little less than 2 [11.5-ounce] jars)
3   large eggs
1   cup sugar
1   cup vegetable oil
2   cups all-purpose flour
1   teaspoon baking soda
1   teaspoon salt
1   teaspoon ground cinnamon
1   teaspoon ground allspice
½   teaspoon ground nutmeg
½   cup buttermilk
1   cup chopped pecans, toasted
1   cup finely chopped prunes
1   to 2 tablespoons chopped fresh rosemary (optional)
Honey-Cheese Frosting
1¾ cups pecan pieces, toasted (optional)
Garnish: fresh rosemary sprigs

Chop large pieces of fig preserves; set aside.

Beat eggs, sugar, and oil at medium speed with an electric mixer until blended. Combine flour and next 5 ingredients; add to sugar mixture alternately with buttermilk, beginning and ending with flour mixture. Fold in fig preserves, 1 cup chopped pecans, prunes, and, if desired, chopped rosemary.

Pour batter into 2 greased and floured 8" round cakepans. Bake at 350° for 45 minutes or until a wooden pick inserted in center comes out clean. Cool in pans on wire racks 10 minutes; remove from pans, and cool on wire racks.

Spread Honey-Cheese Frosting between layers and on top and sides of cake. Press pecan pieces onto sides of cake, if desired. Garnish, if desired. Store cake in refrigerator. **Yield:** 1 (2-layer) cake.

HONEY-CHEESE FROSTING

1½ (8-ounce) packages cream cheese, softened
⅓   cup butter, softened
1½ tablespoons honey
2   cups sifted powdered sugar

Beat cream cheese, butter, and honey at medium speed with an electric mixer just until smooth. Gradually add powdered sugar, beating at low speed just until blended. **Yield:** 3½ cups.

Holiday Fig Cake

ORANGE-PECAN TASSIES

These classic cream cheese tassies are loaded with a buttery pecan pie filling laced with orange. Make and freeze them ahead.

3   large eggs
¾   cup sugar
¾   cup light corn syrup
2   tablespoons grated orange rind
3   tablespoons fresh orange juice
3   tablespoons butter, melted
1   teaspoon vanilla extract
1   cup finely chopped pecans
Pastry Cups

Whisk first 5 ingredients just until blended. Stir in melted butter, vanilla, and pecans. Spoon filling evenly into Pastry Cups, filling three-fourths full. Bake at 325° for 25 minutes or until set. Cool 3 minutes in pans. Remove from pans, and cool on a wire rack. **Yield:** 4 dozen.

PASTRY CUPS

2   (3-ounce) packages cream cheese, softened
⅔   cup butter, softened
2   cups all-purpose flour

Beat cream cheese and butter at medium speed with an electric mixer until creamy. Gradually add flour, beating at low speed just until blended. Wrap dough in wax paper, and chill at least 2 hours.

Divide dough in half. Divide each half of dough into 24 balls. Flatten each ball with palm of your hand, and place in lightly greased miniature (1¾") muffin pans, shaping each into a shell. Cover and chill until ready to fill and bake. **Yield:** 4 dozen.

RUM FUDGE CAKES

A wooden spoon will get you from start to finish with this recipe. The rum flavor permeates these petite fudgy cakes that received our highest rating. Freeze them ahead to simplify party preparation.

1   cup butter
4   (1-ounce) unsweetened chocolate squares
4   (1-ounce) semisweet chocolate squares
1⅓ cups sugar
⅓   cup heavy whipping cream
1½ teaspoons rum extract
3   large eggs
1   cup all-purpose flour
1   cup semisweet mini-morsels
Powdered sugar

Melt butter and 8 ounces chocolate in a heavy saucepan over medium-low heat, stirring often. Remove from heat, and cool completely. Stir in sugar, whipping cream, and rum extract until blended. Add eggs, 1 at a time, stirring until blended after each addition. Gradually fold in flour. Stir in mini-morsels.

Spoon batter into lightly greased miniature (1¾") muffin pans, filling almost full. Bake at 375° for 14 minutes or until a wooden pick inserted in center of cakes comes out clean. Remove to a wire rack to cool. Sprinkle cakes with powdered sugar before serving. **Yield:** 4 dozen.

Orange-Pecan Tassies
Rum Fudge Cakes

Chocolate-Peppermint Bundt Cake
and Mocha Punch

CHOCOLATE-PEPPERMINT BUNDT CAKE

Devil's food cake mix gives you a jump start with this dessert, and chocolate pudding and sour cream make each bite moist.

1   (18.25-ounce) package devil's food cake mix
    (we tested with Betty Crocker)
½   cup sugar
1   (3.9-ounce) package chocolate instant
    pudding mix
1   cup vegetable oil
4   large eggs
1   (8-ounce) container sour cream
1   teaspoon peppermint extract
1   cup sifted powdered sugar
1½ to 2 tablespoons milk
½   cup coarsely crushed hard peppermint candies

Heavily grease and flour a 12-cup Bundt pan. Set aside.
Combine first 7 ingredients in a large mixing bowl. Beat at low speed with an electric mixer just until combined. Beat at high speed 2 minutes. Pour batter into prepared pan.
Bake at 350° for 50 minutes or until a long wooden pick inserted in center comes out clean. Cool in pan on a wire rack 15 minutes; remove from pan, and cool on wire rack.

Place cake on a serving plate. Stir together powdered sugar and enough milk to make glaze a good drizzling consistency. Drizzle glaze over cake, and sprinkle with crushed candies. **Yield:** 1 (10") cake.

MOCHA PUNCH

Chocolate and coffee make a pleasing punch that complements all the sweet treats in this menu.

1   quart chocolate milk
4   cups strong brewed coffee, chilled
1   cup Kahlúa or other coffee-flavored liqueur*
1   (14-ounce) can sweetened condensed milk
1   quart chocolate ice cream
1   quart coffee ice cream
Semisweet chocolate shavings

Combine first 4 ingredients in a large pitcher. Cover and chill. Pour chilled mixture into a large punch bowl. Scoop chocolate and coffee ice creams into punch; stir gently. Sprinkle with chocolate shavings. **Yield:** 4½ quarts.

*Substitute amaretto-flavored nondairy liquid creamer for Kahlúa, or increase coffee to 5 cups.

Tuscan Pork Roast; Potato
Soufflé; and Winter Greens
with Browned Butter, Pine
Nuts, and Golden Raisins

MEDITERRANEAN FAMILY FEAST

Ever dream of holiday travels? This year cook up a culinary adventure. Mediterranean meets the American South in this meal where love of family and food are woven together as one.

Menu for 8

Olive Salad Appetizer

White Bean Soup with Black Pepper Croutons and Truffle Oil

Fennel and Citrus Salad

Tuscan Pork Roast • Potato Soufflé

Winter Greens with Browned Butter, Pine Nuts, and Golden Raisins

Triple Nut Tart • Tiramisù Trifle

OLIVE SALAD APPETIZER

Use premium Greek or Italian olives for the best flavor results. You can make the salad ahead and store it in the refrigerator, but wait until just before serving to stir in mushrooms. Serve trays of extra olives for your family to nibble on while working in the kitchen.

12 green olives, pitted and finely chopped (we tested with Picholine olives)
12 kalamata olives, pitted and finely chopped
1 anchovy, finely chopped
3 tablespoons extra-virgin olive oil
¼ cup diced purple onion
¼ cup finely chopped fresh parsley
2 teaspoons finely grated lemon rind
¼ teaspoon freshly ground pepper
1 (4-ounce) jar marinated mushrooms, drained and finely chopped
1 celery rib, finely chopped
1 garlic clove, minced

Stir together all ingredients (see Note below). Serve with bagel chips. **Yield:** 1¼ cups.

Note: *You can chop the ingredients for this salad in a food processor or mini chopper to save time; however, we prefer the texture and appearance achieved from chopping the ingredients by hand in this recipe.*

Olive Salad Appetizer

WHITE BEAN SOUP WITH BLACK PEPPER CROUTONS AND TRUFFLE OIL

This soup is the splurge course. If you can't find truffle oil, drizzle extra-virgin olive oil over each serving.

1 pound dried great Northern beans
2 tablespoons butter or margarine
1 large onion, chopped
3 celery ribs, chopped
5 garlic cloves, minced
6 cups chicken broth
2 bay leaves
3 sprigs fresh thyme
¼ cup white wine vinegar
1 teaspoon salt
Black Pepper Croutons
White truffle oil or extra-virgin olive oil

Sort and rinse beans; place in a Dutch oven. Cover with water 2" above beans. Bring beans to a boil; cover, remove from heat, and let stand 1 hour. Drain beans; set aside.

Melt butter in Dutch oven over medium heat; add onion, celery, and garlic, and sauté 10 minutes or until golden. Add beans, chicken broth, bay leaves, and thyme; bring to boil. Reduce heat, and simmer, uncovered, 1 hour or until beans are tender, stirring occasionally. Remove from heat. Stir in vinegar and salt. Cool slightly. Remove and discard bay leaves.

Process 3 cups bean mixture in a blender until smooth, stopping to scrape down sides. Stir into remaining soup in Dutch oven. Spoon into soup bowls; top each serving with a Black Pepper Crouton, and drizzle with about 1 teaspoon truffle oil. **Yield:** 7 cups.

BLACK PEPPER CROUTONS
8 (½"-thick) baguette slices
2 tablespoons butter, melted, or olive oil
1 teaspoon freshly ground pepper
¼ teaspoon salt

Brush both sides of baguette slices with melted butter. Place on an ungreased baking sheet. Bake at 400° for 3 minutes. Turn; sprinkle with pepper and salt. Bake 2 to 3 more minutes or until crisp. **Yield:** 8 croutons.

Fennel and Citrus Salad

FENNEL AND CITRUS SALAD

Raw fennel's sweet licorice flavor and crisp texture bring bold notes to this salad of juicy citrus and tangy olives. The dish is known to southern Italy where fennel grows wild.

3   large fennel bulbs (3 pounds)
4   blood oranges or red navel oranges, peeled and sectioned
¼   cup olive oil
¾   teaspoon salt
¼   teaspoon freshly ground pepper
½   cup niçoise olives or pitted kalamata olives
Freshly ground pepper (optional)

   Trim stems and base from fennel bulbs, reserving feathery fronds for garnish. Remove tough outer layer from each bulb. Cut each bulb in half through base. Cut out the small, pyramid-shaped core from each half. Place cored fennel, cut side down, and slice crosswise into 4 thick slices. Slice lengthwise into ¼"-wide strips.

   Combine fennel and orange sections in a serving bowl. Add olive oil, salt, ¼ teaspoon pepper, and ¼ cup olives; toss gently. Pile remaining ¼ cup olives in center of salad. Chop fennel fronds, and sprinkle over salad, if desired. Add more freshly ground pepper, if desired. **Yield:** 6 to 8 servings.

Note: If you can't find fennel, use 1 small head Romaine lettuce, torn. Omit salt and olive oil, and use ½ cup of your favorite vinaigrette.

The Essence of the Mediterranean

•Olive oil, garlic, lemon, fennel, olives, sage, rosemary, oregano, thyme, truffle oil, pine nuts, and Parmesan are all part of the rich culinary history of the Mediterranean Rim. These ingredients are sprinkled throughout this meal, marking it with European authenticity.

•The term Mediterranean Rim designates the collective identity of more than fifteen countries and island nations situated on the Mediterranean Sea. The cuisine and its ingredients from this region of the world have evolved from centuries of travel, trade, and colonization throughout the Mediterranean.

TUSCAN PORK ROAST

Known in Italy as arista (ah-REES-tah), this Tuscan roast is typically seasoned with garlic, pepper, and rosemary. We've added several herbs and a golden gravy spiked with wine.

¼   cup fresh parsley sprigs
¼   cup olive oil
4   garlic cloves
2   tablespoons fresh rosemary leaves
1   tablespoon fresh thyme leaves
1   tablespoon chopped fresh sage
1   teaspoon salt
½   teaspoon freshly ground pepper
1   (4½-pound) boneless pork loin roast, trimmed
3   tablespoons all-purpose flour
2½ cups chicken broth
½   cup dry white wine or chicken broth
1   teaspoon sugar
½   teaspoon salt
1   teaspoon chopped fresh parsley
1   teaspoon chopped fresh thyme
Garnishes: fresh herbs and roasted garlic

Process first 8 ingredients in a food processor or blender 2 minutes or until smooth, stopping once to scrape down sides; set pesto mixture aside.

Butterfly roast by making a lengthwise cut down center of 1 flat side, cutting to within ½" of other side. From bottom of cut, slice horizontally to ½" from left side; repeat procedure to right side. Open roast, and place between 2 sheets of heavy-duty plastic wrap; flatten to ½" thickness, using a mallet or rolling pin.

Spread about two-thirds pesto mixture over roast. Roll up roast, jellyroll fashion, starting with long side, and secure at 2" intervals, using heavy string.

Place roast in a shallow roasting pan; cover with remaining pesto mixture. Bake, uncovered, at 450° for 15 minutes. Reduce heat to 350°; bake 1 hour or until a meat thermometer inserted into thickest portion registers 160°. Remove from pan, reserving drippings in pan; keep roast warm.

Whisk flour into drippings in pan, and cook over medium-high heat 2 minutes, stirring constantly. Add broth and next 3 ingredients; simmer 3 minutes or until thickened. Pour gravy through a wire-mesh strainer into a bowl, discarding solids. Stir in 1 teaspoon each parsley and thyme. Serve gravy with roast. Garnish platter, if desired. **Yield:** 8 servings.

Tuscan Pork Roast

A Family Affair

When the whole family gets involved in preparing the meal, it makes the occasion more memorable. Cooking tips, techniques, and quotes get passed from one generation to the next, and a recipe is assured of staying in the family.

Team up to serve the white bean soup. Top each bowl with a crouton, and give it a light drizzle of luxurious truffle oil.

Fresh fennel is a new vegetable to many cooks. Its texture is crisp like celery, but the flavor hints of licorice. The bulb and feathery tops are most commonly eaten.

Set up food for serving in the kitchen. Isn't that where everyone congregates anyway?

Here's a simple, last-minute way to be sure your guests get a hot meal. Warm dinner plates by running them through the rinse and dry cycle in your dishwasher just before guests arrive.

POTATO SOUFFLÉ

Known in Italy as sformato (sfor-MAH-toa), this dish can be a savory pie, pudding, custard, or soufflé. Our potato version is fairly dense and soufflélike with a crusty top. Cut it into wedges, and add a ladleful of gravy.

2   pounds baking potatoes, peeled and cubed
6   tablespoons butter or margarine
½   cup all-purpose flour
2   cups milk
3   tablespoons butter or margarine
1   large onion, chopped
4   egg yolks, lightly beaten
½   cup freshly shredded Parmesan cheese
1   teaspoon salt
½   teaspoon freshly ground pepper
¼   teaspoon freshly grated nutmeg
1   cup soft breadcrumbs (homemade; see Note on
    page 20), toasted
Garnish: fresh thyme

Cook potato in boiling salted water to cover 25 minutes or until tender; drain well. Return potato to pan; mash with a potato masher.

Melt 6 tablespoons butter in a heavy saucepan over medium heat; whisk in flour until smooth. Cook 1 minute, whisking constantly. Gradually whisk in milk; cook over medium heat, whisking constantly, until sauce is thickened and bubbly. Remove from heat; cool.

Melt 3 tablespoons butter in a large skillet over medium heat; add onion, and sauté 10 minutes or until tender and browned.

Stir together mashed potato, onion, white sauce, beaten egg yolks, and next 4 ingredients. Mash with potato masher until smooth.

Butter a 9" x 3" springform pan. Add ½ cup breadcrumbs, tilting to coat bottom and sides of pan. Freeze 1 minute to set crumbs. Spoon potato filling into pan. Top with remaining ½ cup breadcrumbs.

Bake, uncovered, at 400° for 50 minutes or until set. Cool 15 minutes before removing sides of pan. Garnish, if desired. Serve warm. **Yield:** 8 to 10 servings.

WINTER GREENS WITH BROWNED BUTTER, PINE NUTS, AND GOLDEN RAISINS

Mild greens, such as Swiss chard and kale, taste best when cooked quickly, just until tender. Here they're lightly dressed with browned butter, toasted nuts, and raisins.

2½ pounds fresh Swiss chard, kale, or spinach
¼   cup butter
½   cup golden raisins
¼   cup pine nuts
1   teaspoon salt
½   teaspoon freshly ground pepper

Remove and discard ribs from Swiss chard. Rinse chard with cold water; drain and coarsely chop.

Melt butter in a sauté pan or Dutch oven over medium heat; cook 2 minutes or until butter begins to brown. Add raisins and pine nuts; sauté 2 to 3 minutes or until pine nuts are golden. Gradually add chard. Sauté 3 minutes or until greens are wilted. Add salt and pepper; toss well. Transfer to a serving bowl. **Yield:** 6 cups.

TRIPLE NUT TART

Three types of nuts crown this tart that's reminiscent of pecan pie in flavor.

½   (15-ounce) package refrigerated piecrusts
1   cup sugar
½   cup light corn syrup
¼   cup butter or margarine
4   large eggs, lightly beaten
1   teaspoon vanilla extract
¼   teaspoon salt
½   cup pecan halves
½   cup macadamia nuts
⅓   cup blanched whole almonds, toasted

Unfold piecrust, and press out fold lines. Fit piecrust into a greased and floured 9½" round tart pan with a removable bottom. Prick bottom of piecrust with a fork. Bake at 400° for 10 minutes or until golden. Cool on a wire rack. Reduce oven temperature to 325°.

Stir together sugar, corn syrup, and butter in a saucepan; cook over medium heat until butter melts and sugar dissolves, stirring often. Remove from heat; cool slightly. Add eggs, vanilla, and salt; stir well. Stir in nuts. Spoon filling into crust.

Bake at 325° for 55 minutes or until set. Cool on a wire rack. Serve with unsweetened whipped cream or ice cream. **Yield:** 1 (9") tart.

TIRAMISÙ TRIFLE

Two steps will assure your success with this famed Italian "pick-me-up" dessert—packing the ladyfingers snugly in the dish so you're sure to use them all and using every drop of the coffee-rum syrup to soak them.

16   ounces mascarpone cheese*
1   (8-ounce) package cream cheese, softened
1   cup whipping cream
⅓   cup sifted powdered sugar
2   teaspoons vanilla extract
1½ cups whipping cream, whipped
1   cup (6 ounces) semisweet chocolate morsels, melted
1¼ cups fresh brewed strong coffee, cooled (we tested with a French roast)
⅓   cup dark rum
3   (3-ounce) packages ladyfingers
2   (1-ounce) white chocolate squares

Beat first 5 ingredients at high speed with an electric mixer 45 seconds or just until blended. Gently fold in whipped cream. Divide mixture into 2 portions. Fold melted chocolate into 1 portion. Set both mixtures aside.

Stir together coffee and rum.

Split ladyfingers in half. Arrange enough ladyfingers to cover bottom of a 3-quart trifle dish or other glass bowl. Soak ladyfingers with coffee mixture. Top with half of chocolate cheese mixture. Add another layer of ladyfingers; soak with coffee mixture. Top with half of cream cheese mixture. Repeat layers with remaining ladyfingers, coffee and cheese mixtures, ending with cream cheese mixture. Cover and chill trifle 8 to 24 hours. Grate white chocolate using a vegetable peeler, and pile shavings in center of trifle just before serving. **Yield:** 8 servings.

*As a substitute for mascarpone cheese, combine 2 (8-ounce) packages cream cheese, ⅓ cup sour cream, and ¼ cup whipping cream; beat well. Use 2 cups for recipe, reserving remainder for other uses.

Triple Nut Tart

Tiramisù Trifle
Triple Nut Tart

45

CHRISTMAS AT THE CABIN

Take a walk in the woods, build a roaring fire, give thanks, and look forward to this hearty meal in a setting filled with rustic Christmas charm.

Menu for 6

Forest Mushroom Soup

Pear Salad with Hazelnuts and Sage

Fig-Glazed Quail

Cornbread Dressing with Bacon and Pecans

Skillet Red Cabbage

Baked Fudge Cups with Orange Cream

Invite friends to the table with these bright metal baskets brimming with fresh greenery.

FOREST MUSHROOM SOUP

Three kinds of mushrooms lend meaty texture to this ultra-rich soup that gets your meal off to a warming start.

1   (8-ounce) package sliced fresh mushrooms
4   ounces fresh shiitake mushrooms, stems removed
1   cup finely chopped onion
3   garlic cloves, minced
3   tablespoons butter or margarine, divided
½   cup dry white wine
3   tablespoons all-purpose flour
4   cups chicken broth
1   teaspoon salt
¼   teaspoon freshly ground pepper
1   cup whipping cream
7   ounces fresh oyster mushrooms, coarsely chopped
1   cup coarsely chopped fresh shiitake mushrooms
      (2 ounces)
Freshly ground pepper

Finely chop sliced mushrooms and 4 ounces shiitake mushrooms, or pulse mushrooms in a food processor 5 or 6 times.

Sauté finely chopped mushrooms, onion, and garlic in 2 tablespoons butter in a large saucepan over medium-high heat 8 minutes or until tender. Add wine; simmer 3 minutes or until wine has almost evaporated.

Combine flour and ½ cup broth, stirring until smooth; add to soup. Stir in remaining 3½ cups broth, salt, and pepper. Bring to boil; reduce heat, and simmer, uncovered, 10 minutes. Stir in whipping cream. Return soup to a boil; reduce heat, and simmer 1 minute. Remove from heat.

Sauté chopped oyster mushrooms and 1 cup shiitake mushrooms in remaining 1 tablespoon butter in a large skillet over medium-high heat 3 to 5 minutes or until golden; stir into soup. Season to taste with freshly ground pepper. **Yield:** 7 cups.

Forest Mushroom Soup

PEAR SALAD WITH HAZELNUTS AND SAGE

*The crisp, mild bite of pears is balanced with tangy cranberries,
toasted hazelnuts, and earthy sage in this beautiful, fresh salad.*

½	cup hazelnuts
½	cup crème fraîche (see Note)
2	tablespoons white balsamic vinegar
1	tablespoon honey
½	teaspoon salt
3	cups loosely packed gourmet mixed salad greens
4	Asian pears or other pears, cut into wedges
½	cup dried cranberries
2	tablespoons fresh sage leaves, cut into thin strips

Place hazelnuts on an ungreased baking sheet. Bake at
350° for 15 minutes or until skins split. Place hazelnuts in
a colander. Rub hazelnuts briskly with a kitchen towel to
remove skins; discard skins. Coarsely chop hazelnuts.

Whisk together crème fraîche and next 3 ingredients.
Arrange salad greens and pear wedges on salad plates.
Drizzle evenly with dressing; sprinkle with hazelnuts,
cranberries, and sage. **Yield:** 6 servings.

*Note: To make your own crème fraîche, stir together ½ cup
whipping cream and 1 tablespoon buttermilk. Cover and let
stand at room temperature 8 hours. Then store in refrigerator
up to 10 days.*

Cornbread Dressing with Bacon and Pecans, Fig-Glazed Quail, and Skillet Red Cabbage

FIG-GLAZED QUAIL

A maple glaze thickened with pureed figs paints a golden coating on these quail and becomes a scrumptious sauce, too.

10   dried figs, coarsely chopped
1   tablespoon grated orange rind
½   cup fresh orange juice
2   tablespoons butter or margarine
½   teaspoon ground cinnamon
2   tablespoons maple syrup
3   cups chicken broth, divided
12   quail, dressed*
2   teaspoons salt, divided
¾   teaspoon pepper, divided
2   to 3 tablespoons vegetable oil
2   tablespoons cornstarch
¼   cup water

Stir together first 6 ingredients in a small saucepan. Add 1 cup chicken broth. Bring to a boil; cover, reduce heat, and simmer 10 minutes. Cool 5 minutes. Process mixture in a food processor 1 minute or until pureed. Set aside.

Truss each quail with heavy string or by inserting a wooden pick through end of one leg, tip of breast, and end of other leg. Sprinkle quail with 1 teaspoon salt and ½ teaspoon pepper.

Heat oil in a large skillet over medium-high heat until hot. Fry quail, in batches, 5 minutes on each side or until browned. Place quail, breast side up, on a baking sheet or roasting pan. Brush with ⅓ cup fig puree.

Bake, uncovered, at 475° for 15 to 16 minutes or until golden. Arrange quail on a platter, remove string or picks, and cover to keep warm.

Combine remaining fig puree, 2 cups broth, 1 teaspoon salt and ¼ teaspoon pepper in a saucepan. Bring to a boil; reduce heat and simmer, uncovered, 1 minute. Pour mixture through a wire-mesh strainer into a bowl, discarding solids. Return sauce to saucepan. Combine cornstarch and water, stirring until smooth. Stir into sauce; cook over medium heat until sauce thickens. Serve sauce with quail. **Yield:** 6 servings.

*If you can't find quail, use 6 large skinless, boneless chicken breast halves. Sprinkle with 1 teaspoon salt and ½ teaspoon pepper. Heat oil in a large skillet as directed above. Brown chicken in hot oil on both sides. Place chicken on a baking sheet; brush with ⅓ cup fig puree. Bake, uncovered, at 475° for 15 to 20 minutes or until chicken is done.

CORNBREAD DRESSING WITH BACON AND PECANS

Pecans and bacon are great tossed into this holiday dressing.

Buttery Cornbread
6 bacon slices
4 celery ribs, finely chopped
1 large onion, finely chopped
6 cups torn day-old bread (6 slices)
⅔ cup chopped pecans, toasted
1 large egg, lightly beaten
2 tablespoons light brown sugar
1 tablespoon chopped fresh or 1 teaspoon rubbed sage
1 teaspoon salt
½ teaspoon freshly ground pepper
3 to 4 cups chicken broth (see box at right)

Prepare Buttery Cornbread; cool and crumble. Set aside.

Cook bacon in a large skillet until crisp; remove bacon, drain on paper towels, reserving drippings in skillet. Crumble bacon, and set aside. Sauté celery and onion in bacon drippings in skillet 10 minutes or until tender.

Combine crumbled cornbread, bacon, sautéed onion mixture, bread, and remaining ingredients in a large bowl; stir well. Spoon dressing into a 13" x 9" baking dish. Bake, uncovered, at 375° for 45 minutes or until golden. **Yield:** 10 servings.

BUTTERY CORNBREAD

1 cup all-purpose flour
¾ cup cornmeal (not cornmeal mix)
2 tablespoons sugar
1 tablespoon baking powder
½ teaspoon salt
1 large egg, lightly beaten
¾ cup milk
½ cup butter or margarine, melted
2 tablespoons butter or shortening

Combine first 5 ingredients in a large bowl. Combine egg, milk, and ½ cup melted butter; stir with a wire whisk. Add egg mixture to dry ingredients, stirring just until dry ingredients are moistened. Set aside.

Melt 2 tablespoons butter in an 8" cast-iron skillet over medium-high heat. Pour batter into skillet. Bake at 425° for 20 to 25 minutes or until a wooden pick inserted in center comes out clean. **Yield:** 1 (8") round cornbread.

The Big Dressing Debate

When it comes to Southern dressing, there's no question what bread to use—it's got to be predominantly cornbread. The debate begins with how much broth to add. For most people, the answer is easy. They like it just like Mom used to make it. If you like your dressing drier and crustier, use 3 cups broth in the recipe at left. Use 4 cups for a moister dressing.

SKILLET RED CABBAGE

Every menu needs an easy recipe like this skillet side dish. Once you've done the slicing and shredding, the recipe needs very little attention.

1 large purple onion, sliced and separated into rings
¼ cup butter or margarine, melted
½ teaspoon salt
½ teaspoon pepper
1 medium-size red cabbage (2 pounds), cored and coarsely shredded
¼ cup red wine vinegar
3 tablespoons sugar

Sauté onion in butter in a large deep skillet or Dutch oven until tender. Sprinkle with salt and pepper. Cook onion 15 more minutes or until caramelized, stirring often.

Toss shredded cabbage with vinegar and sugar. Gradually add to caramelized onion in skillet, stirring well. Cover and cook over medium heat 25 minutes or until cabbage is tender. Serve warm. **Yield:** 6 servings.

BAKED FUDGE CUPS WITH ORANGE CREAM

Somewhere between rich chocolate pudding and decadent fudge pie is the best way to describe this dessert. It's gooey, and the Orange Cream is just the light contrast needed.

2 cups sugar
¾ cup cocoa
½ cup all-purpose flour
5 large eggs
1 cup plus 2 tablespoons butter or margarine, melted
2 teaspoons vanilla extract
1⅓ cups chopped pecans, toasted
Orange Cream
Garnish: orange zest

Combine first 3 ingredients. Add eggs; beat at medium speed with an electric mixer until smooth. Add butter and vanilla, beating well. Stir in pecans.

Spoon mixture into 8 greased 6-ounce custard cups or ramekins (see Note). Place cups in a large roasting pan; add hot water to pan to depth of 1". Cover pan with aluminum foil, and bake at 300° for 1 hour. Uncover pan, and remove cups from water. Let stand 10 to 15 minutes. Serve warm with Orange Cream. Garnish, if desired. **Yield:** 8 servings.

Note: *If you don't have custard cups, baked fudge can be prepared in a greased 9″ square pan. Cover and bake in water bath 1 hour and 15 to 20 minutes. Spoon into dessert dishes.*

ORANGE CREAM

½ cup whipping cream
¼ cup sifted powdered sugar
1 tablespoon orange liqueur or fresh orange juice
¼ teaspoon grated orange rind

Beat whipping cream at medium speed until foamy. Gradually add powdered sugar, beating until soft peaks form. Fold in liqueur and orange rind. Cover and chill until ready to serve. **Yield:** 1 cup.

Baked Fudge Cups with
Orange Cream

A big tree filled with family-favorite ornaments is the essence of Christmas decorating. Here, the cabin theme is carried out in the gift wrappings, as well. Kraft paper-wrapped packages, corrugated gift bags, and burlap bundles are adorned with rustic-colored raffia and paper and burlap ribbons. To purchase similar wrappings, see page 171.

A treasured Santa collection sets the tone for the cabin's woodsy mantel. The evergreen garland unifies the individual elements—the Santas, tall candleholders, and stockings—while adding the welcome sight and aroma of fresh greenery.

▲ Three small vine wreaths make a bold decorating statement hanging from a band of twigs. The twig band can be purchased from a crafts store, or you can wire together twigs that you find scattered in your own backyard. Decorate the vine wreaths with an assortment of berries, greenery, even small pieces of fruit, nuts, and pinecones. Use floral wire, floral picks, or a hot-glue gun to attach embellishments to the wreaths. Wire the wreaths to the twig band; then cover the wire with a crisp ribbon and bow.

▲ Bright metal baskets filled with fresh greenery clippings and berries bring Christmas cheer to dining chairs. To keep the clippings fresh for several days, place a small piece of moistened floral foam inside a plastic bag. Place the foam and bag in the metal basket. Stick stems in the foam.

▲ Oversize pinecones wired to rope add a festive surprise when used as a drapery tieback. Embellish the pinecones with ribbons and cording tassels, as desired. To order pinecones and tassels, see page 171.

CHAPTER 2

DECORATING IDEAS

Capture the magic of the season with festooned mantels, flower-bedecked doors, and lush centerpieces that make your home say "Merry Christmas" every minute of the day.

ANTEBELLUM ELEGANCE

*Leave the main road, go down the winding driveway
to Ruff House, and step back in time.*

Not far from downtown Atlanta, this grand Southern home sits just off a busy road, insulated from neighborhoods and shopping centers by eleven acres of land. Philip Ivester grew up in Ruff House, which was named for the owner who built it in 1851, and now he and his wife, Lanier, call it home.

Lanier likes to decorate the house true to its period, so each Christmas season, she watches the movie *Little Women*, pausing and poring over the holiday scenes for decorating inspiration. "The movie takes place during the Civil War, and I like to get ideas from the March family,"

Lanier says. "Philip and I always thought we were born 150 years too late. We like doing things the way they did them back then."

The Ivesters use simple decorations for the exterior of their home—although it's no easy task for Philip to climb outside the upstairs windows to attach the wreaths. An evergreen garland embellished with pinecones drapes over the door and along each side, curving gently around the lanterns. Bright bows of red ribbon accent the garland, all of the wreaths, and the candlestands that line the front walk.

◀ A TIMELESS ARRANGEMENT

The rich, dark wood in the library demands a refined decor, so Lanier primarily uses fresh materials to embellish this room. A full garland of boxwood, Fraser fir, and pine crowns the mantel; cranberries and lady apples add perks of color and depth. Butterscotch candles introduce a new hue and provide varying heights to an otherwise horizontal arrangement. Since the chimney needs to be renovated and can't be used, Lanier fills the fireplace with magnolia leaves.

The mantel scarf offers an innovative twist on the tradition of hanging stockings: the mantel scarf's pockets provide roomy places to hold gifts and treats. For patterns and instructions, see page 168.

▲ SIMPLE AND NATURAL

In keeping with Christmas tree decorations of the mid-1800s, most of Lanier's ornaments are fresh, hand-made, and from the kitchen. She makes gingerbread men and pipes royal icing snowflakes. Other ornaments have sentimental value, such as a miniature of the church where Philip proposed marriage or the ballerina that represents one of Lanier's many interests. She also strings popcorn and cranberry garlands; after the holidays, Lanier recycles her garlands as food for birds and squirrels. She reuses a few favorite items from year to year, such as a colorful paper chain made from archival paper that won't fade or disintegrate. The round tree skirt is simply tacked up at intervals and trimmed with ribbons, bells, and tassels for added interest.

▲ A RING OF LEAVES

Although festive, the colors in the velvet leaves wreath aren't strictly reminiscent of Christmas, so the wreath can be displayed year-round, if desired. Assembly is easy: wrap ribbon around a wreath form; then overlap and glue the velvet leaves to it. Tack a ribbon hanger to the back. For instructions on making velvet leaves, see page 166.

WRAPPED IN TOILE ▶

The staircase may seem an unlikely place for a wreath, but it fits just fine in the front hall at Ruff House. To make a similar wreath, wrap strips of toile around a form, and secure with straight pins. Wire clay pots filled with rosemary, sage, and hypericum berries to the wreath; then wrap small strips of gingham around each pot. This wreath is attached to the newel with wire, which is then covered with a large strip of gingham.

TRADITIONAL SETTING

Clipping greenery from her yard ranks as one of Lanier's favorite parts about decorating for Christmas. Not much in the dining room is left untouched: Lanier slips wreaths of boxwood around candles on the sideboard, wires cedar sprigs to the chandelier, and tucks holly into empty spaces around the sugared fruit in the centerpiece. To add drama, a red satin bow is tied to the chandelier and the ends of the bow stream down onto the centerpiece and trail across the table.

In simple touches, Lanier groups fresh fruits on the mantelpiece and combines them with candles and greenery to form a tasteful and balanced arrangement. Pears perch in two candlesticks, clementines and lady apples fill Revere bowls, and cranberries crest Jefferson cups.

Her great-grandmother always included sugared fruit in her Christmas decorations, and Lanier continues the tradition in her home.

▲ VELVET REVELRY

Hang these no-sew ornaments on a tree; or to showcase their detail and beauty, display them on stacked glass cake stands as shown here. Though the ornaments are made from a kit, they reinforce the antebellum ambience of the home's other decorations. To order a kit, see page 171.

◄ CHRISTMAS CORNUCOPIAS

These genteel decorations make inventive favors for guests. Lanier makes them from remnants of drapery fabric. For each one, she forms a cone and then seals the seam with glue and covers it with trim. Peppermints, fruits, and berries fill the cornucopias; a jingle bell hangs from each tip.

DRESSING UP WITH STYLE ▲

Fanciful velvet pillows accent a sofa or a chair with a touch of Christmas cheer. Although these pillows require some sewing, they are still easy to construct. For each, simply cut the imprinted velvet and fabric using the provided pattern, stitch the pieces together, and stuff the pillow. Draw a heavy thread, anchored by a button, through the center of the pillow, and pull to cinch; embellish with a tassel. For pattern and instructions, see page 162.

▲ LETTER-PERFECT ACCESSORIES

Going the extra step of adding an initial to packaging shows that a great deal of thought went into the process. Instead of embroidering monograms on gift bags, sew buttons in the shape of letters. Make sacks from left-over fabric, and run a drawstring or ribbon through the top to close it.

MANTEL MAJESTY ▶

Even the shallow ledge above the fireplace in the kitchen is dressed for Christmas. Each year, Lanier dries orange and apple slices in her oven to make a kitchen garland. During the eight hours of baking, the fruits fill the entire house with a Christmas fragrance. Lanier further embellishes the mantelpiece with fresh cuttings of evergreen and holly, candles, nuts, and cranberries. Greenery wired to the sconces and the small painting includes them in the decorations, as well.

Lanier created her own holly alphabet to embroider initials on her family's handmade stockings. The larger stockings belong to Philip and Lanier, and their cats have the smaller ones.

Silver candelabra, mixed china, and fresh fruits and flowers bring elegance and sophistication to this dining room tablescape—perfect for a celebration.

A HOME FOR THE HOLIDAYS

Take a tour of The Caroline House, and see how one church celebrates the Christmas story through decorating.

Each holiday season, women from Briarwood Presbyterian Church in Birmingham, Alabama, decorate The Caroline House, the church's guest house, and then open its doors for tours. "It's a comfortable environment where our ladies can bring their friends," says Cheri Bachofer, coordinator of Women's Ministries at Briarwood. "The purpose is to invite friends and to share the spirit of Christmas."

Several groups of ladies from the church "adopt" various rooms in the house and decorate them to the hilt according to their Christmas-related themes.

LET HEAVEN AND NATURE SING

The words to a favorite Christmas carol inspired the sitting room's decorations. This room reflects nature's harmony through the fresh greenery that frames the window, and the birds, the dried flowers, and the embellished balls that adorn the tree. Candles, cookies, and a comfortable chair make this a truly natural spot for lingering.

To bring a little of the outdoors into your holiday decorating, glue dried fruits, moss, or berries onto Styrofoam balls. Nestle the balls in a basket or on a pillow of moss.

The hutch's shelves brim with fragrant greenery, beaded berry balls, and a rustic crèche. A book open to a favorite Christmas story and a shepherd lamp complete the simple arrangement.

A vignette comprised of a woodsy Santa and potted paperwhites tied with ribbons adds a festive touch to a corner.

WE THREE KINGS

This dining room decor symbolizes the pomp and circumstance of Christmas and represents a table setting suitable for royalty. Sparkly jewel tones and luscious fabrics and textures lend a regal look to the setting. An abundance of gold braided rope, ribbons, and fabric adds to the majesty of the tablescape.

An arrangement of flowers and greenery crowns each chair, honoring guests at the table. To adorn your chairs with style, wire a piece of garland around the top of each chair, and tuck flowers and greenery sprigs in for extra color and fullness.

Glass ornaments and ribbons stream from the chandelier, creating a visual extension of the treasure chest centerpiece.

▲ STELLAR CREATIONS

Star-shaped floral topiaries line the mantel in the dining room. To make a topiary, cut a star-shaped base from floral foam, and fill it with flowers and greenery. Support the star with a dowel or straight stick pushed firmly into a container filled with floral foam or Styrofoam.

◄ A WELL-BALANCED ARRANGEMENT

Instead of having only florals in an arrangement, experiment using fresh vegetables and fruits. Roses, hypericum berries, brussels sprouts, apples, and lemons partner to make an unexpected yet delightful fresh grouping.

EXQUISITE ENTRY ▶

A scented candle and fragrant flowers create an inviting atmosphere for the home's entrance. The height of the amaryllis complements the candlestick and the mirror for a stunning vertical combination in the foyer. For a bright splash of color in your decorating, plant amaryllis bulbs four to eight weeks before Christmas.

COURTYARD CHARM

Like a quaint village from an earlier time, eight Tudor-style cottages stand in the middle of a bustling city, yet are worlds away. At The Courtyard—houses face each other across a central square—holiday decorating takes a fascinating turn.

▲ ALL IS CALM

Nothing says Christmas like a garlanded tree framed in a window. The window box planted with ivy and pansies contributes to the heartwarming vignette and mirrors the colors on the tree. Though each Courtyard house has its own distinctive decorations, the abundant use of natural materials is a common characteristic.

◀ SURROUNDED BY CEDAR

A canopy of evergreen branches greets guests with a refreshing foresty scent. Vivid blue gazing globes nestled in the flowerbeds, tiny blue twinkle lights in the evergreen clematis surrounding the door, and soft white luminarias on the steps are a departure from conventional decorations yet prove there's more than one way to announce the season.

A WARM WELCOME ▶

Beautifully lush greenery showcases the glowing coach light and is repeated in the mossy wreath on the front door. A base of moistened floral foam secured with wire around the lamp keeps the evergreen clippings fresh for ten days to two weeks.

▲ SPRIGHTLY SPHERE

An oversize grapevine ball is a fitting complement to the flowing grapevine garland seen in the photo at right. A handful of greenery wired to the top of the ball softens its woody appearance and dresses it simply and naturally for the holidays.

◀ ALL IS BRIGHT

Houselike luminarias illuminate the stairs leading to the courtyard and create a wee town of their own. Evergreen and grapevine garlands entwine to wrap the banister and lamppost, enhancing the natural materials theme.

DISTINCTIVE DETAILS ▶

Twists and loops of grapevine wind up and over the door, creating a lively frame for this front entrance. Soaking the vine prior to arranging makes it more pliable and easier to position. Evergreen, berries, and bows wired to the garland add a rich focal point.

SAY IT WITH FLOWERS

Greet your holiday guests with bouquets of fresh flowers.
Floral foam keeps the arrangements looking good for over a week.

A FRESH WELCOME

Save your wreath for next year. This season, go all out with wire baskets overflowing with colorful blooms. Any style of flat-backed basket will work, and you can find plenty of blooming plants at garden shops and grocery stores. On this front door, two baskets are wired together to extend the welcome.

If your basket doesn't have a plastic liner, use a heavy-duty zip-top plastic bag to hold moistened floral foam. Fill the basket with evergreen clippings, flowers, berries, and ribbons for a beautifully natural showpiece.

STARS OF THE SEASON

Carnations take center stage in this colorful door display. Inexpensive and widely available, these blooms will last seven to ten days when stems are kept moist in a base of floral foam.

For each star, cut the foam in the desired size of star. Wrap it with chicken wire. Line the edges of the star with ribbon to help hold the shape, using pins to secure the ribbon (see photo at left).

Clip the flowers, leaving a 1" to 1½" stem on each. Push the stems into the star form, completely covering the front of the star. Pin a wide ribbon to the back of the star to use as a hanger.

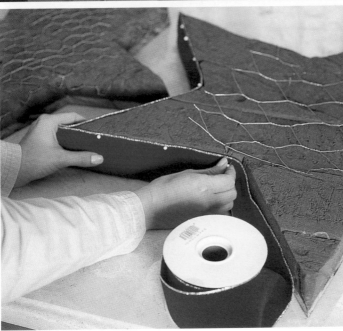

TABLETOP TABLEAUX

A bare tabletop offers an enticing invitation to creative decorating. Whether you choose a berried topiary, a miniature evergreen forest, or a tiny village of brightly glowing paper houses, you'll relish the fun of filling your home with the ideas on these pages.

◀ BERRIED TREASURES

Tree-shaped Styrofoam topiaries wrapped round and round with grapevine are the basis for these berry-laden decorations. Generous clusters of berries and seeded eucalyptus are wired to floral picks and tucked in among the vines. Loops of brightly colored ribbon, secured with floral wire, stick easily into the foam to add bursts of color and to fill in any gaps.

The topiary form we used has a Styrofoam base that fits easily into the bucket. Tuck clippings in around the base. ▲

An inexpensive metal bucket, painted in a complementary hue, makes a perfect topiary container. Use masking tape to mark off areas to paint stripes, or stencil holiday-motif designs, such as this snowflake, on the sides. ▲

To add a collar of pansies, place the topiary in a plastic pot with drainage holes, fill in with potting soil, and plant the pansies around the base of the topiary. Line the decorative metal bucket with a plastic bag to catch the runoff when watering the pansies. Set the plastic pot inside the bucket. ▶

PETITE PAPER VILLAGE

These diminutive paper houses, reminiscent of stately Southern homes, cast a spirited sparkle. Warm light from the votive candles placed inside the houses spills from the windows and makes a most inviting setting. Shown here as a dining table centerpiece, the houses are equally attractive arranged on a sideboard, a coffee table, or a mantel.

For diagrams and instructions, see page 163.

Let It Snow

This wintry vignette allows you to enjoy the frosty beauty of a snowy scene from a cozy armchair. A fairyland of lustrous ivory candy canes and glistening Christmas tree candles is showered with fluffy everlasting snowflakes. Neatly wrapped packages, all in white, form a backdrop for this enchanting tablescape.

◀ MERRY MOODS

Make the most of your tabletop setting by layering elements with a common theme. On this holiday table, a grouping of woodland Santas sets a mood that is heartily echoed by rustic pillar candles encircled with seeded eucalyptus wreaths and fragrant rosemary topiaries. Using a quilt instead of a traditional tablecloth cinches the bucolic theme.

AN ENCHANTING FOREST ▲

This fetching assortment of potted evergreens fills the senses with the fragrances of the Yuletide. Mini cypress trees, ivy topiaries, and tall spikes of rosemary form the base of this arrangement, which is embellished with luxurious gift boxes wrapped in varying shades of green. This design proves that any combination of items can come together easily when you establish a consistent creative thread, such as fresh plants and the use of a similar color.

CAPTIVATING COLLECTIONS ▶

The peace of a pastoral homeplace is evoked with this grouping of wooden farm animals and buildings. The tiny wreath and snow-flocked trees suggest the season and make this well-loved family heirloom a favorite feature of each year's holiday trimmings. Adorn your own cherished collectibles with evergreen clippings, berries, ribbons—anything Christmassy—to create a charming tabletop decoration.

Outdoor Adornments

A backyard table offers yet another chance to spread holiday cheer. Here, simple birdhouses relate harmoniously to their sylvan setting. Potted evergreens, red berries, festive candles, and a vine garland winding among the birdhouses give the grouping a sense of unity and design. Though set up for the holidays, this tableau can be enjoyed throughout the winter.

FRESH & FANCY CENTERPIECES

*While you're at the market, pick up some extra vegetables
and fruits to make colorful centerpieces.*

Visit your grocery's produce section for a wealth of materials to create bright and festive centerpieces for your holiday table and sideboard. Take a cue from the ideas presented on these pages, and then use your imagination to create one-of-a-kind arrangements. Moistened floral foam is a good base for holding the materials and will preserve the flowers' freshness for several days.

◀ CLASSICAL INSPIRATION

Red roses, pears, grapes, pomegranates, and lady apples form a glorious base for a vine wreath in a decorative urn. Floral picks hold all the pieces securely in place. Don't forget about ornate outdoor planters when choosing containers for your arrangements. The urn used here, for example, contributes a stately air to the overall appearance of the grouping.

A BOUNTIFUL TOWER ▶

The colors of Christmas are represented in all their glory in this fresh topiary made from the season's brightest fare. Green and red bell peppers, tangerines, kumquats, limes, star fruit, lady apples, and red grapes fill the holiday decoration to overflowing. Bundles of asparagus, evergreen, and a handful of berries at the top add points of interest to the treelike shape.

Blocks of floral foam wrapped with chicken wire form the foundation. Before you begin, soak the foam in water, and allow it to drain. Secure the stack of blocks with long floral picks. Use shorter floral picks to attach the produce to the foam.

▲ JOYFUL ABUNDANCE

This opulent table decoration allows you to use any combination of flowers and vegetables you like.
The size of the arrangement is determined by the number of floral foam blocks wrapped with chicken wire that you use as a base. Protect your tabletop by placing plastic trash bags underneath the arrangement. Position pillar candles between the foam blocks, and fill in with fresh flowers, greenery clippings, and produce.

CHRISTMAS PEAR TREE ▶

Pretty partridges perch among pears on stacked cake stands to form a whimsical centerpiece. If you don't have cake stands, use clear glass plates with sturdy drinking glasses as spacers. Line up pears along the outside of the plates, and nestle plump partridge ornaments here and there. Encircle the top and bottom with greenery sprigs, and place votive candles around the tree to add sparkling highlights.

▲ SCENTED CANDLEHOLDERS

These fruity candleholders are equally at home in the kitchen or in the dining room. To assemble each, thread citrus fruits on a bamboo skewer (available at grocery stores). Twine sprigs of rosemary and cranberries strung on floral wire around the fruits.

For the base, use heavy-duty scissors to cut squares of sheet metal into star-burst shapes. (Sheet metal for crafting is available at crafts and hardware stores in rolls or in small sheets.) Top each point with a cranberry. To insert a candle into the top of the fruit, use an apple corer to create a hole, or insert a pointed, plastic candleholder (available at crafts or floral supply stores).

VASES OF PLENTY ▶

Cranberries, kumquats, and lady apples fill fluted glass vases with wonderful scents and colors, providing ideal holders for tall tapers. For a special trim, wrap strands of raffia around the candles. Knot the strands at the bottom. As a safety precaution, don't light candles wrapped with raffia. The ones pictured were lit for photography only.

When burning candles, follow these safety tips from the National Candle Association.

- Never leave a burning candle unattended.
- Keep candles out of the reach of children and pets.
- Trim wicks prior to each use.
- Keep candles away from drafts and flammable objects.

WOODLAND CHANDELIER

Embellishing the chandelier in this outdoor setting sets a festive mood.
These tips make decorating a chandelier easy—indoors or out.

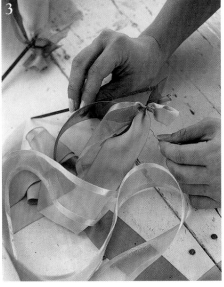

1. Encircle the chandelier with pre-made wreaths. Here, a seeded eucalyptus wreath is wired to the hanging supports. Attach a floral foam wreath to the bottom. Make a cut in the wreath to fit it around the fixture.

2. Fill the wreaths with evergreen clippings, berries, and flowers for an abundant appearance. Wire bunches together with floral picks for easy insertion.

3. Wind ribbons around the supports, and tie long streamers from the base of the chandelier. Wire loops together with floral picks, and insert into the wreaths.

CHAPTER 3

HANDMADE CHRISTMAS

*The season has arrived for crafting handmade
tokens of affection for family and friends.
But who has time? You do! Turn the
page for a sleighful of quick ideas.*

DECORATIONS

Felt is so inexpensive and easy to work with that you'll love creating these treats to add a holiday touch to every corner of your home.

SIMPLE STOCKINGS ▲

Fashion lots of these stockings to use as ornaments and chair-back decorations or to hold flatware at the holiday table. The embossed felt used to make the stockings pictured features motifs that are easy to cut out and use for embellishments. Or cut a shape of your own design, such as a star, a tree, or a snowflake, and sew or glue it to the stocking front. For the cuff, take a cue from the photo, and cut a zigzag design, a checkerboard look with slits for weaving ribbon, or a scalloped edge. Trim the cuffs with buttons or ribbons. For a stocking and cuff pattern, see page 165. For felt ordering information, see page 172.

CHRISTMAS CONE ▶

Filled with greenery and shiny candy canes, this cone easily brings holiday color to unexpected places. To keep greenery fresh, place a zip-top bag filled with wet paper towels inside the cone, and then add the greenery.

For the cone, cut a triangle from felt. Cut a triangular inset from a contrasting color of felt; sew or glue it to the front of the cone. Trim the inset with buttons. Sew or glue the cone together along the sides. Fold the top over for a cuff, and attach a ribbon for a hanger. For the tassel, fold several lengths of ribbon in half, and wrap with a ribbon to secure. Tack the tassel to the point of the cone.

PILLOW ENVELOPES

Stitch up these felt pillow covers for quick-and-easy additions to your seasonal decorating plans. For each, cut two pieces of felt large enough to hold the desired pillow, allowing enough on the back piece to fold over for a flap. Use pinking shears to trim the edges, if desired. Stitch the front and back pieces together along the sides and the bottom. Refer to the photo for ideas on cutting a decorative edge on the flap and for trimming with buttons, ribbons, and felt cutouts. Stuff the envelope with the pillow, and fold the flap toward the front.

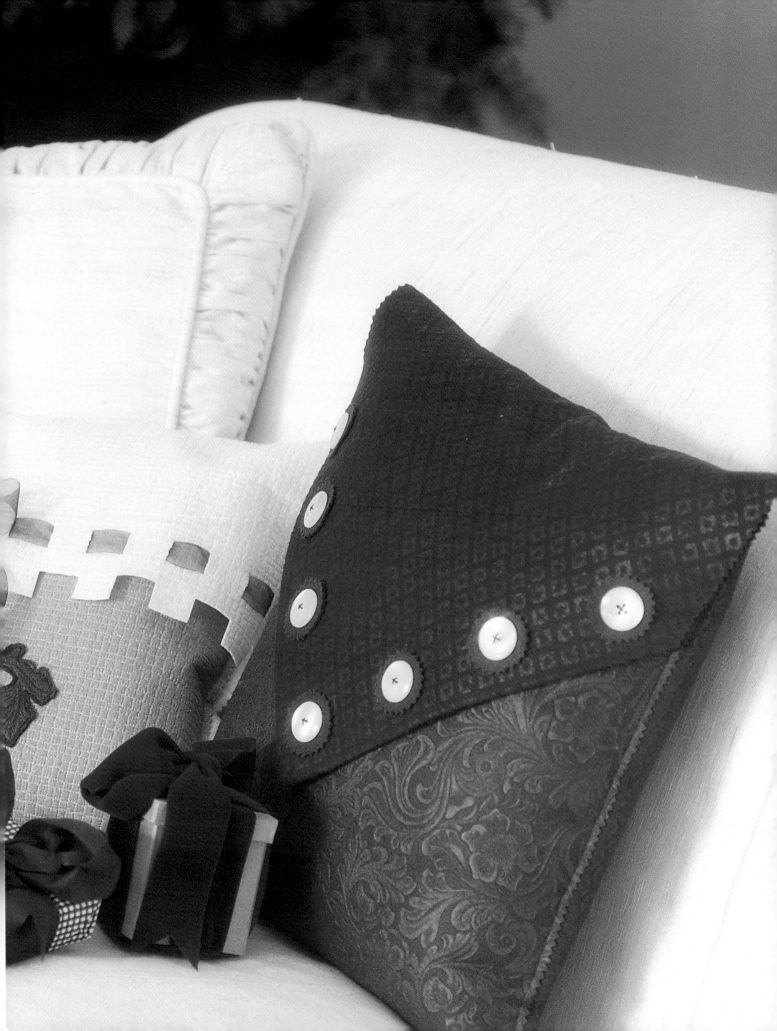

GIFTS

*These handcrafted presents show your generous spirit,
and you'll actually have fun making them!*

◀ FELT-WRAPPED BOOKS

Turn an ordinary photo album or address book into a handsome gift. Trim a piece of felt large enough to completely wrap around the book or album you want to cover. Wrap snugly with the felt, smoothing out any wrinkles. Fold the edges to the inside, using craft glue to secure the felt. For a neat finish, cut another piece of felt, perhaps in a complementary color, to line the inside covers of the album or the book. Glue in place.

Use the snowflake pattern on page 166 or the alphabet on page 167 to cut a felt embellishment for the cover. Glue in place.

GIFT BAGS WITH MATCHING TIES ▲

Plush felt bags are quick to assemble and make a fabulous impression when filled with Christmassy trinkets. For each, handstitch the felt back and front pieces together, using contrasting thread for a fresh-looking finish. Repeat that color in the ribbon ties. Glue or sew felt cutouts to the ribbon ends.

CORDING COASTERS

Shape a batch of these attractive coasters to give as a hostess gift. Just stack several together, and tie with a bow. To make each coaster, coil a length of cording into a flat circle, hot-gluing or handstitching to hold the cording in place. Turn the ends toward the back. Sew on a delicate bead for a decorative finish.

FANCY PHOTO HOLDERS

Take a trip to the hardware store for unfinished wooden drawer knobs to form the bases for fun photo holders. Paint the wooden balls with fanciful designs. After the paint dries, drill a tiny hole in the top of each knob, just large enough to insert a wire that you've strung with colorful beads. (A drop of glue in the hole will help hold the wire in place.) Twist and bend the wire in any shape you like to make the top, and secure it to the beaded stem.

BEADED BEAUTIES

Let your imagination be your guide with designs that you make by stringing beads on craft wire and then twisting the wire around votive holders. Once you get started, it's like child's play. In fact, kids will love this activity. For holiday sparkle on a larger scale, try a similar treatment around a large pillar candle.

GREETINGS

Surprise loved ones with clever Christmas greetings
that offer a new twist on the old standard.

CARD-IN-A-BOX

Use tiny gift boxes and tin containers to make remarkably inventive Christmas cards. Unopened, the boxes resemble small gift packages. But when each top is lifted a cheery message unfolds. To enjoy the cards all season, nestle the box lids in the Christmas tree, and allow the letter blocks to flow artfully down the branches. For instructions, see page 164. To order rubber stamps, see page 172.

ACCORDION-FOLD GREETING

This holiday card unfolds to make a lovely Christmas decoration. Use any cardstock-weight paper, and draw or stamp a design on the card. The card pictured gets its artsy look from resist paper, which features an "invisible" design printed on the paper that is revealed in various shadings when covered with ink. For instructions, see page 164. To order resist paper, cardstock paper, and rubber stamps, see page 172.

WRAPPINGS

Gifts embellished this wonderfully make what's inside the boxes seem doubly delightful.

SEVEN SENSATIONAL SOLUTIONS

How can you wrap gifts with great style and not spend a fortune? The suggestions on these four pages use an assortment of snippets and trinkets—many from your sewing box and fabric stash—to create wrappings that show how much you care.

1 Glue on a fabric initial to personalize a gift. A candy cane adds sweetness.

2 Spell a name with small fabric initials. Trim printed papers with pinking shears to form a bright background.

3 Cut a shape from construction paper, and "sew" together with skinny ribbon. Stuff with tiny surprises.

4 Tie small ornaments to a thin cord, knot the cord around the bow, and let the ornaments trail down the sides of the box.

5 Use scraps of felt or fabric instead of wrapping paper.

6 Go for the unusual: use computer clip art or an old magazine clipping for a one-of-a-kind tag embellishment.

7 Glue shaped buttons and charms on a printed paper cutout for a dashing adornment.

FOUR FANCY FINISHES

Think outside the box—the traditional wrapped box that is—by adding out-of-the-ordinary accents.

1 Wind strands of craft pearls around a box, and knot them in place. Used this way, the pearls serve the same function as ribbon.

2 Create a swirling box-top decoration with wire leaf garland.

3 Use wire-edged ribbon if a fluffy bow is what you want.

4 Add a pinafore to your package by wrapping a strip of decorative paper across the top of the box. Hold the paper in place with string or ribbon.

FIVE DAPPER DETAILS

Enhance the dramatic impact of your wrappings by sticking with one primary color. Here are some other tips to add spark to your wraps.

1 Stack several small gifts, and tie together. Add a color-coordinated handmade tag.

2 Coordinate rickrack with a sticker and a vintage stamp on a holiday gift card.

3 Plump up the bow by introducing a new element, such as the miniature winter scarf shown here. A candy cane tucked in is always welcome.

4 Create an instant winter scene with three little buttons and snowflake stickers glued to a square card.

5 Wrap a tissue-covered box with waxed or glassine (semi-transparent) paper for an elegant finish.

COOKIE HOUSES

Start a new Christmas tradition; build these cookie houses as a family project. Each house is glued together with icing and embellished with an assortment of candies. They look good enough to eat, but these houses are for decoration only.

Cookie house expert Susann Montgomery-Clark shares her best tips and techniques to get you started.

All three cookie houses—the Red Barn, the Country Church, and Santa's Workshop—are built similarly with graham crackers. The basic buildings are 5" squares and stand about 6" high.

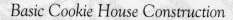

Basic Cookie House Construction

1. To assemble base of house, pipe icing in a square on cardboard base. Pressing short edges of 2 crackers together with icing, place crackers on a corner of icing on cardboard, and hold in place 1 minute. Reinforce inside corner seam with icing, using finger.

2. Pipe icing along both short edges of third cracker wall of house. Attach to 1 of 2 crackers in place; hold 1 minute.

3. Pipe icing along 1 short edge of a fourth cracker wall. Attach to complete the square. Hold in place 1 minute.

SANTA'S WORKSHOP COOKIE HOUSE

9 whole chocolate graham crackers
Nonedible Icing (page 124)
Decorations: candy canes, red cinnamon candy,
    hard peppermint candy disks, soft chocolate
    candy roll, fat peppermint sticks, large green and red
    gumdrops, semisweet chocolate mini morsels
1 (9") white cardboard cake round, sturdy paper plate, or
    other cardboard base
Additional cardboard
Cotton ball
Artificial snow (see Note)
Fresh greenery clippings

To Make Workshop Windows and Door: Place 2 whole graham crackers, back side up, on a flat surface (these will be sides of workshop). Pipe outline for windows with icing. Fill in windows with icing in a crisscross pattern (see photo 1, at right). Cut curved ends of candy canes with scissors and fit onto windows; cut straight pieces of candy cane to fit at base of windows (see photos 2 and 3, at right).

Place another whole graham cracker, back side up, on flat surface. Pipe outline for door in center. Fill in door with icing; spread smooth with a small spatula. Add cinnamon candy as doorknob. Cut 1 curved end of a candy cane; fit over left side of door. Cut another curved end of a candy cane; fit over right side of door. Pipe icing over door to cover seam.

To Make Workshop Base: Start near 1 edge of cardboard (to leave room for a pathway), and squeeze a line of icing ¼" thick in a 5" square. (Use a pencil to sketch this out first, if needed.) This square will hold the workshop's 4 walls firmly to the cardboard base.

Squeeze icing along 1 short edge of 1 cracker with windows. Press cracker against 1 short edge of a plain whole cracker (the back of workshop). Place crackers on a corner of icing on cardboard. Gently hold 2 walls in place 1 minute or until set. Reach into the inside corner seam of 2 walls and reinforce the seam with more icing, using your finger (see photo 1, at left). Repeat procedure to attach the other side and front of workshop, 1 cracker at a time (see photos 2 and 3, at left). Reinforce inside corner seams with icing, using finger. Set workshop aside to dry completely (at least 1 hour) before adding roof. Meanwhile, decorate crackers for roof.

To Make Roof: Cut 1 graham cracker in half lengthwise using a serrated knife and a gentle sawing motion. Place half of cracker next to long side of a whole cracker, measure them together, and cut out cardboard to match size. Glue 1½ crackers to cardboard, using icing. Let dry. This will be 1 long side of roof. Repeat procedure to make other side of roof, using remaining cut graham cracker piece and another whole cracker.

Place 2 cardboard-backed roof pieces on a flat surface. Pipe icing to cover cracker side of roof pieces. Smooth icing with spatula or knife. Decorate with rows of peppermint disks, covering crackers completely. Set aside to dry.

Pipe icing across top of side walls of workshop and across 1 long edge of 2 roof pieces. Gently position roof pieces in place on top of side walls. Hold 2 roof pieces in place 1 minute. (Roof and walls should line up exactly.)

Pipe icing on top of roof; add chocolate candy roll for chimney. Hold in place 1 minute. Pipe a little icing on top of candy roll; add cotton ball.

Cut remaining 2 graham crackers into wide triangles, using a serrated knife and a gentle sawing motion. On back of large triangles, pipe a small circle of icing. Press peppermint disks into icing. Set triangles aside to dry.

Pipe icing around all edges of 2 decorated triangles. Attach triangles to front and back of roof to complete the workshop. Hold pieces in place 1 minute.

To Add Finishing Touches: Pipe more icing onto roof, corners of workshop, windows, and window sills. While squeezing icing in bag, slowly pull bag away to form icicles. Pipe icing icicles to cover any gaps in roof. Attach fat peppermint sticks to 4 corners of workshop using icing. Pipe icing onto gumdrops; place around workshop as snow-covered bushes. Pipe outline of path with icing, and fill in with icing; sprinkle with mini morsels. Sprinkle artificial snow around workshop, covering cardboard completely. Add greenery.

Note: *Find artificial snow at most crafts stores.*

Santa's Workshop Windows

1. Pipe outline for windows with icing. Fill in windows with icing in a crisscross pattern.

2. Cut curved ends and straight pieces of candy canes with scissors.

3. Fit curved candy canes onto windows. Finish window sills with straight pieces of candy.

Country Church Cookie House

9 whole graham crackers
Nonedible Icing (page 124)
Decorations: crushed assorted flavors roll candies, silver
    dragées (see Note), miniature chocolate candy bars,
    sunflower kernels
1 (9") white cardboard cake round, sturdy paper plate,
    or other cardboard base
Additional cardboard
1 sugar cone ice cream cone
Artificial snow (see Note page 121)

To Make Church Windows and Doors: Place 4 whole graham crackers on a flat surface. Frost one side of each cracker with icing; smooth with a spatula. Draw lines through icing to resemble siding on a house (see photo 1, below).

Decorate 2 frosted crackers with stained glass windows for the sides of the church. Using icing, pipe outline of each window, and then fill in with icing. Sprinkle crushed assorted roll candies inside each window to resemble stained glass. Press candy gently to adhere. Pipe as desired around windows, and decorate with small silver dragées. Set aside to dry.

Decorate 1 frosted graham cracker as the front of the church. Using icing, pipe outline of double doors, and then fill in with icing. Trim miniature chocolate candy bars to fit as doors. Press chocolate doors into icing. Pipe 2 dots of icing onto doors; press 2 large silver dragées into icing. Pipe as desired around doors, and decorate with dragées.

To assemble base of church, follow directions from Santa's Workshop (paragraphs 3 and 4 on page 121).

To Make Roof and Steeple: Cut 1 graham cracker in half lengthwise using a serrated knife and a gentle sawing motion. Place half of cracker next to long side of a whole cracker, measure them together, and cut out cardboard to match size. Glue 1½ crackers to cardboard using icing (see photo 2, below). Let dry. Repeat procedure to make other side of roof, using remaining cut cracker piece and another whole cracker.

Place 2 cardboard-backed roof pieces on a flat surface. Pipe icing as desired to cover cracker side of roof pieces. Decorate with small silver dragées. Set aside to dry.

Pipe icing across top of side walls of church and across 1 long edge of 2 roof pieces. Gently position roof pieces in place on top of side walls. Hold 2 roof pieces in place 1 minute. (Roof and walls should line up exactly.)

Break off little pieces from wide end of sugar cone to fit cone on roof. Pipe icing onto cone. Decorate with a silver dragée on top. Set aside to dry. Apply icing onto bottom of cone. Gently place cone on roof for steeple. Hold in place 1 minute.

Cut remaining 2 graham crackers into wide triangles, using a serrated knife and a gentle sawing motion (see photo 3, below). Frost 1 side of each large triangle with icing; smooth icing with a spatula. Using a knife, draw lines through icing to resemble siding. On 1 frosted triangle, outline desired shape for a stained glass window using icing. Fill in with icing, and sprinkle with crushed candies. Press candies gently to adhere. Set triangles aside to dry.

Pipe icing around all edges of 2 frosted triangles. Attach to front and back of roof. Hold pieces in place 1 minute. Pipe icing to fill in gaps above triangles.

To Add Finishing Touches: Pipe icing along roof edges and corners of church; immediately apply silver dragées, if desired, using tweezers. Pipe outline of path with icing and fill in with icing; place sunflower kernels inside path to create walkway. Press to adhere. Apply silver dragées to outline of path, using tweezers. Sprinkle artificial snow around church, covering cardboard completely.

Note: We used a box containing 3 sizes of nonedible silver dragées. See sources on page 172 for ordering information.

Country Church Walls and Roof

1. Using a knife, draw lines through icing to resemble siding on a house.

2. Glue 1½ crackers to cardboard with icing. This will be 1 long side of roof.

3. Cut 2 crackers into wide triangles, using a serrated knife and a gentle sawing motion. These will be front and back of roof.

RED BARN COOKIE HOUSE

Nonedible Icing (recipe at right)
Red paste food coloring
9 whole graham crackers
1 (9") cardboard cake round, sturdy paper plate, or other
    cardboard base
Additional cardboard
Frosted mini shredded whole wheat cereal biscuits
Pine straw
Small pine cones

To Make Barn Base: Divide icing into 2 portions. Tint 1 portion with food coloring until desired shade of red.

Place 2 whole graham crackers on a flat surface (these will be the sides of the barn). Frost 1 side of each cracker with red icing; smooth icing with a spatula. Using a knife, draw lines through icing to resemble siding on a house. Let dry.

Decorate frosted crackers with windows for sides of barn. Using white icing, pipe outline of each window.

Place 2 more crackers on a flat surface (these will become the stacked front of the barn). Cut 1 cracker into a wide triangle, using a serrated knife and a gentle sawing motion. Place triangle next to long side of other cracker, measure them together, and cut out cardboard to match size. Glue 2 stacked crackers to cardboard using icing. Let dry. Repeat procedure for the back of the barn, using 2 more crackers. Let dry. Frost cracker side of both stacked pieces with red icing. Smooth icing with a spatula. Using a knife, draw lines through icing to resemble siding. Let dry.

Decorate 1 stacked frosted cracker as the front of the barn. Using white icing, pipe outline of doors, and then fill in each door with an "X." Let dry.

To assemble barn base, use red icing, and follow directions from Santa's Workshop (paragraphs 3 and 4 on page 121). (Barn will look different, because the front and back pieces are two-story at this point.)

To Make Roof: Cut 1 graham cracker in half lengthwise, using a serrated knife and a gentle sawing motion. Pipe white icing to cover 1 side of each cracker half. Apply 2 rows of frosted cereal to each cracker half, starting at bottom of cracker and working up. Let dry. Pipe white icing to cover 1 side of 2 more whole crackers. Apply 4 rows of frosted cereal to each whole cracker, starting at bottom of cracker and working up. Let dry.

To Construct Roof: Pipe red icing across top of side walls of barn and across all 4 edges of 1 cereal-topped half cracker roof piece. Gently position half cracker piece in place, sitting on a side wall. Hold in place 2 to 3 minutes. Repeat with remaining cereal-topped half cracker roof piece. Pipe red icing onto all 4 edges of 2 whole cereal-topped crackers. Position both pieces onto roof, allowing them to lean in on each other.

To Add Finishing Touches: Pipe white icing between roof shingles and along roof edges to fill in gaps where roof pieces meet. While squeezing icing in bag, slowly pull bag away to form icicles. Place barn on a wooden board, if desired. Scatter pine straw and small pine cones around barn.

Nonedible Icing

This icing is intended for decorating purposes only because it contains uncooked egg whites. If you'd like to use edible icing, purchase meringue powder at cake-decorating or crafts stores, and prepare icing according to package directions.

2 egg whites
½ teaspoon cream of tartar
1 (16-ounce) package powdered sugar
Liquid food coloring (optional)
1 teaspoon water (optional)
Heavy-duty zip-top plastic bags

Beat egg whites at high speed with an electric mixer until frothy. Add cream of tartar and beat until soft peaks form. Gradually add powdered sugar, beating until blended. Icing should be consistency of pasty glue; it should stick to a spoon, and not pour. Add food coloring, if desired. Add water, if needed, to reach desired consistency. (If you add food coloring, you won't need to add water.)

Spoon icing into heavy-duty zip-top plastic bags; seal bags. Secure with rubber bands near top to prevent leaks. Just before ready to use, cut a tiny hole (⅛" to ¼") in corner of each bag for piping. (If you'd rather use a decorating bag and metal tips, use a small round tip.)

Note: *1 recipe of Nonedible Icing yields enough to make 2 cookie houses.*

CHAPTER 4

HOLIDAY RECIPES

*Good food and friends make the
season merry. Let these holiday recipes lure
you to linger at the table.*

HOLIDAY SOUPS & STEWS

Sip your way through our selection of wintry soups. Think of them as make-ahead holiday meals. Then enhance your bowl with one of our bread pairings: crisp croutons, buttery biscuits, or braided yeast bread.

Curried Pumpkin Soup
with Spicy Pumpkin Seeds

CURRIED PUMPKIN SOUP WITH SPICY PUMPKIN SEEDS

Begin your Christmas feast with this luxuriously rich soup served in pumpkin shells. It makes an impressive appetizer, especially when garnished with Spicy Pumpkin Seeds, which you won't be able to quit eating.

8   mini pumpkins (1½ to 2 pounds each)
1½ cups chopped onion
1   Golden Delicious apple, peeled and chopped
2¼ cups chicken broth
2   cups half-and-half
1   teaspoon curry powder
½   teaspoon salt
Sour cream
Spicy Pumpkin Seeds

Remove stem end of pumpkins by slicing about 1½" off top. Scoop out seeds; reserve seeds of 2 pumpkins. Place pumpkins and tops, cut side down, on greased large baking sheets. Bake at 375° for 35 to 45 minutes or just until tender. Cool 30 minutes. Gently scoop out most of pulp from all 8 pumpkins, leaving enough pulp in 6 shells so they are intact for serving. Set aside 2¼ cups pulp.

Place onion and apple in a large saucepan; add 1¼ cups chicken broth. Bring to a boil; cover, reduce heat, and simmer 30 to 40 minutes or until very tender. Process pumpkin pulp and onion mixture in a food processor until smooth. Return mixture to saucepan; add remaining 1 cup chicken broth, half-and-half, curry powder, and salt. Cook over medium heat just until soup comes to a simmer. (Do not boil.)

Place pumpkin shells on individual serving plates. Spoon soup into each shell. Dollop with sour cream, and sprinkle with Spicy Pumpkin Seeds. Add pumpkin tops, if desired. **Yield:** 8 cups.

SPICY PUMPKIN SEEDS

Seeds from 2 mini pumpkins (about ¾ cup)
1   tablespoon olive oil
½   teaspoon salt
½   teaspoon ground cumin
¼   teaspoon ground red pepper
¼   teaspoon paprika

Remove excess fiber and pulp from seeds, and pat dry with paper towels. Stir together seeds and oil. Combine salt and remaining ingredients; sprinkle mixture over seeds, tossing well. Spread seeds in a single layer on an ungreased baking sheet. Bake at 300° for 35 to 40 minutes, stirring often, until roasted and crisp. **Yield:** ¾ cup.

HAM AND LENTIL STEW

This hearty stew recipe was inspired by the annual spiral sliced holiday ham that usually needs a new destiny by the end of its first week in the refrigerator. Choose from slow cooker or stovetop directions.

2   leeks
1   meaty ham bone from a spiral sliced ham
4   carrots, sliced into ½" pieces
½   green bell pepper, chopped
1   cup dried lentils
⅓   cup chopped fresh parsley
1   (14½-ounce) can diced tomatoes with green pepper and onion, undrained
1   (14½-ounce) can beef broth
1   (10½-ounce) can beef consommé
1½ cups water
¼   teaspoon freshly ground pepper

Remove root, tough outer leaves, and tops from leeks, leaving 2" of dark leaves. Slice leeks; rinse well, and drain.

Place ham bone in a 5-quart electric slow cooker. Add leeks and remaining ingredients. Cook, covered, on HIGH 1 hour; reduce heat to LOW, and cook 6 hours. Remove ham bone; cool slightly. Cut off meat and chop. Discard bone; return meat to stew. **Yield:** 10 cups.

Dutch Oven Method: Combine all ingredients in a large Dutch oven. Bring to a boil; cover, reduce heat, and simmer 1½ hours. Remove ham bone, cut off meat, and continue as directed above.

Christmas Cheer
Want a beautifully simple centerpiece in seconds? Transform an antique transferware tureen into a vase and display branches of red berries and greenery. Just place a soaked block of florist foam into the tureen; then anchor branches into the foam.

Cranberry-Apple
Soup

Steak and Two Potato
Soup

Chicken Cacciatore
Stew

CRANBERRY-APPLE SOUP

Savor the sweet, tart hint of apple flavor in this velvety smooth, brilliant red soup. A drizzle of heavy cream and a few Cinnamon-Sugar Croutons make it dessert, good warm or chilled.

1   (12-ounce) package fresh or frozen cranberries, chopped (see Note below)
3   cups water
6   whole cloves
3   Golden Delicious apples, peeled and coarsely chopped
2   (3") cinnamon sticks
1   teaspoon grated orange rind
²/₃ cup sugar
2   tablespoons cornstarch
2   tablespoons water
6   tablespoons heavy whipping cream
Cinnamon-Sugar Croutons (page 134)

Stir together cranberries, 3 cups water, and cloves in a large saucepan. Bring to a boil; reduce heat and simmer, uncovered, 5 minutes.

Strain cranberry mixture through a wire-mesh strainer lined with a coffee filter into a bowl; set aside. Meanwhile, combine apple and cinnamon sticks in saucepan; add water to cover. Bring to a boil; reduce heat, and simmer, uncovered, 20 to 25 minutes or until apple is very soft. Drain; discard cinnamon sticks.

Process apple, ½ cup reserved cranberry liquid, and orange rind in a food processor until smooth. Return apple mixture to saucepan; stir in remaining reserved cranberry liquid and sugar. Cook over medium heat until sugar dissolves, stirring often.

Stir together cornstarch and 2 tablespoons water until smooth. Stir cornstarch mixture into soup. Cook 2 minutes or until soup is slightly thickened. Serve warm or chilled.

Ladle soup into bowls. Drizzle cream into soup; gently swirl cream with a knife. Top with Cinnamon-Sugar Croutons. **Yield:** 4½ cups.

Note: *You can chop cranberries easily by pulsing them 3 or 4 times in a food processor.*

STEAK AND TWO POTATO SOUP

Men fancy this soup. Tender chunks of steak are joined by potatoes and Cheddar cheese in a creamy base. One-Hour Wild Rice-Parmesan Rolls (page 135) make a nice dipping bread.

1½ pounds lean boneless round steak, cut into 1" pieces
¾ teaspoon salt
½ teaspoon pepper
2 to 3 tablespoons vegetable oil
2 celery ribs, sliced
1 medium onion, chopped
3 large garlic cloves, minced
3 cups chicken or beef broth
2 cups water, divided
3 Yukon Gold potatoes, unpeeled and cut into
   ¾" cubes (about 1¼ pounds)
1 medium-size sweet potato, peeled and cut into
   ¾" cubes (about 8 ounces)
2 tablespoons all-purpose flour
½ cup whipping cream
1½ cups (6 ounces) shredded sharp Cheddar cheese
1 tablespoon chopped fresh parsley (optional)
1 tablespoon chopped fresh chives (optional)
Freshly ground pepper

Sprinkle beef with salt and pepper; brown beef in batches in hot oil in a Dutch oven over medium-high heat. Remove beef from pan; set aside. Add celery and onion to pan; sauté 5 minutes. Add garlic; sauté 30 seconds. Return beef to pan; add broth and 1¾ cups water. Bring to a boil; cover, reduce heat, and simmer 1 hour. Add Yukon Gold potato to pan; cook, covered, 10 minutes. Add sweet potato; cook 20 minutes or until beef and potatoes are tender.

Combine flour and remaining ¼ cup water, stirring until smooth. Gradually stir into meat mixture; cook, uncovered, 5 minutes. Stir in cream; cook 5 more minutes. Stir in cheese and, if desired, herbs; cook 1 minute or until cheese melts. Sprinkle each serving with freshly ground pepper just before serving. **Yield:** 10 cups.

CHICKEN CACCIATORE STEW

Mushrooms, onions, tomatoes, and wine typify cacciatore. Taste them all in this chicken stew enhanced with pasta and fragrant herbs. Add a salad, and your meal's complete.

2 tablespoons olive oil
4 chicken leg-thigh combinations, skinned and separated
1 large onion, chopped
3 carrots, sliced
1 large green bell pepper, chopped
2 garlic cloves, minced
1 (8-ounce) package sliced fresh mushrooms
1 (32-ounce) carton chicken broth
2 (14.5-ounce) cans diced tomatoes with roasted garlic,
   undrained (we tested with Contadina)
1 cup water
½ cup white wine (we tested with Chardonnay)
⅓ cup fresh oregano leaves
3 tablespoons fresh thyme leaves
3 bay leaves
½ teaspoon salt
½ teaspoon freshly ground pepper
4 ounces uncooked spaghetti, broken into 3" pieces
Freshly shredded Parmesan cheese
Garlicky Herb Croutons (page 134)

Pour oil into a large Dutch oven. Brown chicken in hot oil over medium-high heat 4 minutes on each side; transfer chicken to a platter.

Sauté onion, carrot, green pepper, and garlic in Dutch oven 5 minutes or until tender. Add mushrooms; cook, stirring often, 3 minutes. Add chicken, chicken broth, and next 8 ingredients. Bring to a boil; cover, reduce heat, and simmer 30 minutes. Add spaghetti, and cook, covered, 12 more minutes. Discard bay leaves. Sprinkle stew with Parmesan cheese. Serve with Garlicky Herb Croutons. **Yield:** 12½ cups.

Turkey and Navy Bean Chili

The smoky essence of Southwest cuisine infuses this soup. Charred chiles, tomatillos, and roasted garlic are theme flavors you'll savor. Try Chili-Cheese Croutons (page 134) on top.

1   (16-ounce) package dried navy beans
4   fresh poblano chile peppers
4   tomatillos, husks removed
1   large garlic bulb
2   tablespoons olive oil, divided
1   medium onion, chopped
1   (32-ounce) carton chicken broth
1   (14½-ounce) can chicken broth
5   cups chopped cooked roasted turkey (we tested with Louis Rich Oven Roasted Turkey Breast)
1   tablespoon ground cumin
½   teaspoon salt
¼   teaspoon freshly ground pepper
½   cup chopped fresh cilantro or parsley
Sour cream
Chili-Cheese Croutons (page 134)

Place beans in a large Dutch oven; add water 2" above beans. Bring to a boil. Boil 2 minutes; cover, remove from heat, and let stand 1 hour. Drain; return beans to pan.

Cut peppers in half lengthwise; discard seeds and membranes. Place peppers, skin side up, on an aluminum foil-lined baking sheet, and flatten with palm of hand. Add whole tomatillos to baking sheet. Broil 5½" from heat 15 to 20 minutes or until blistered and charred, turning tomatillos once.

Place peppers in a heavy-duty zip-top plastic bag; seal and let stand 10 minutes to loosen skins. Peel peppers; coarsely chop peppers and tomatillos.

Meanwhile, cut off pointed end of garlic; place garlic on a piece of aluminum foil, and drizzle with 1 tablespoon oil. Fold foil to seal. Bake at 425° for 30 minutes; cool. Squeeze pulp from garlic cloves; set aside.

Sauté onion in remaining 1 tablespoon hot oil until tender; add to beans. Add peppers, tomatillos, chicken broth, and next 4 ingredients. Bring to a boil; cover, reduce heat, and simmer 1 hour and 45 minutes or just until beans are tender. Stir in cilantro and roasted garlic. Simmer 10 more minutes. Ladle chili into bowls; top with sour cream and croutons. **Yield:** 12 cups.

Black-Eyed Pea and Sausage Soup

A great recipe for New Year's day, this simple soup simmers the traditional good luck peas along with smoky sausage and spicy salsa. Cornmeal Biscuits are a must for dunking.

1   pound smoked sausage, sliced
2   teaspoons vegetable oil
1   large onion, chopped
3   carrots, coarsely chopped
3   garlic cloves, minced
2   celery ribs, chopped
1   large green bell pepper, chopped
4   cups frozen black-eyed peas (about 1½ [16-ounce] packages)
3   (14½-ounce) cans beef broth
1   (14½-ounce) can diced tomatoes with basil, garlic, and oregano, undrained
1   (16-ounce) jar chipotle-flavored salsa (we tested with Pace)
½   teaspoon salt
¼   teaspoon pepper

Cook sausage in oil in a large Dutch oven, stirring until it browns. Remove sausage, reserving drippings in pan. Add onion and next 4 ingredients; sauté over medium-high heat 8 minutes or until vegetables are tender. Stir in sausage, peas, broth, and tomatoes; bring to a boil. Cover, reduce heat, and simmer 35 minutes. Stir in salsa, salt, and pepper; simmer 10 more minutes. **Yield:** 10 cups.

Cornmeal Biscuits with Sage Butter

Enjoy these biscuits and butter with Black-Eyed Pea and Sausage Soup or with an old-fashioned vegetable dinner.

1½   cups all-purpose flour
½   cup yellow cornmeal
2   teaspoons baking powder
½   teaspoon baking soda
¼   teaspoon salt
⅛   teaspoon ground red pepper
⅓   cup cold butter, cut into pieces
⅔   cup buttermilk
⅓   cup sour cream
Sage Butter

Black-Eyed Pea and Sausage Soup,
Cornmeal Biscuits

Stir together first 6 ingredients in a large bowl. Cut butter into flour mixture with a pastry blender until crumbly; add buttermilk and sour cream, stirring just until dry ingredients are moistened. Turn dough out onto a lightly floured surface; knead 4 or 5 times.

Pat or roll dough to ¾" thickness; cut with a 2¼" biscuit cutter, and place on a lightly greased baking sheet.

Bake at 425° for 10 minutes. Serve with Sage Butter. **Yield:** 1 dozen.

SAGE BUTTER

½ cup butter or margarine, softened
1½ tablespoons chopped fresh sage

Beat butter vigorously with a wooden spoon until creamy; stir in sage. Cover and chill. Serve at room temperature. **Yield:** ½ cup.

Cornmeal Biscuits
with Sage Butter

CHILI-CHEESE CROUTONS

Recommended with Turkey and Navy Bean Chili (page 132).

16 (½" thick) French baguette slices
½ cup (2 ounces) finely shredded Monterey Jack cheese
⅓ cup butter or margarine, softened
2½ teaspoons chili powder

Place baguette slices on a baking sheet. Bake at 375° for 5 minutes, turning slices once.

Stir together cheese, butter, and chili powder. Spread cheese mixture onto croutons. Bake at 375° for 7 more minutes. **Yield:** 8 servings.

CINNAMON-SUGAR CROUTONS

Best served with Cranberry-Apple Soup (page 130).

8 (½" thick) French bread slices, cubed
½ cup butter or margarine, melted
1 tablespoon sugar
¾ teaspoon ground cinnamon

Place bread cubes in a large zip-top plastic bag; add melted butter. Seal bag, and shake to coat. Combine sugar and cinnamon; add to bag, reseal, and toss well. Arrange cubes on an ungreased baking sheet or jellyroll pan. Bake at 325°, stirring occasionally, for 28 minutes or until crisp and dry. **Yield:** 4 cups.

GARLICKY HERB CROUTONS

Serve with Chicken Cacciatore Stew (page 131) or any other savory soup.

⅓ cup butter or margarine
2 garlic cloves, minced
4 (¾" thick) French bread slices, cubed
1 tablespoon chopped fresh or 1 teaspoon ground sage
1 tablespoon chopped fresh or 1 teaspoon dried oregano
1 tablespoon chopped fresh or 1 teaspoon dried basil
½ teaspoon salt

Melt butter in a skillet. Add garlic, and sauté just until fragrant. Remove from heat; cool. Place bread cubes in a large zip-top plastic bag; add garlic butter. Seal bag, and shake to coat. Add herbs and salt to bag. Reseal bag, and toss well. Arrange cubes on an ungreased baking sheet or jellyroll pan. Bake at 375°, stirring occasionally, for 10 to 12 minutes or until crisp. **Yield:** 2 cups.

A Spoonful of History

Tablespoons   Cream Soup Spoons   Bouillon Spoons

The spoon is thought to be the oldest of the basic eating utensils. The common oval-shaped tablespoon came along in the seventeenth century and remains the most widely used type of spoon. By the late nineteenth century, spoons multiplied in all shapes and sizes to satisfy the desires of Victorian England. There was a round-bowl spoon for cream soups, a smaller round-bowl spoon for bouillon or consommé, and a host of other specialty spoons, which today are considered collector's items.

Jalapeño-Cheese Braids

Team with Turkey and Navy Bean Chili (page 132) or Ham and Lentil Stew (page 129).

5   cups bread flour, divided
2   (¼-ounce) envelopes active dry yeast
2   teaspoons sugar
1   teaspoon salt
1   cup water
1   cup milk
3   tablespoons butter
1   large egg
1¼ cups (5 ounces) shredded sharp Cheddar cheese, divided
1   cup sliced pickled jalapeño peppers, drained and divided
¾   cup (3 ounces) sharp Cheddar cheese, cubed
¼   cup butter or margarine, melted

Combine 2 cups flour, yeast, sugar, and salt in a large mixing bowl.

Combine water, milk, and 3 tablespoons butter in a saucepan; heat until butter melts. Remove from heat, and cool to 120° to 130°. Gradually add hot liquids to flour mixture, beating at medium speed with an electric mixer. Beat 2 minutes. Add egg; beat 1 minute. Stir in 1 cup shredded cheese and ¾ cup peppers. Using a wooden spoon, gradually stir in enough remaining flour to make a soft dough.

Turn dough out onto a well-floured surface; add cubed cheese, and knead dough until smooth and elastic (about 8 minutes). Place in a well-greased bowl.

Cover and let rise in a warm place, free from drafts, 40 minutes or until doubled in bulk. Punch dough down; divide in half. Shape each portion into 3 ropes; place ropes on a lightly greased large baking sheet. (You can bake loaves on 1 large baking sheet or on 2 smaller pans, if necessary.) Braid ropes, pinching ends under. Place remaining ¼ cup peppers between ropes. Cover and let rise in a warm place 20 minutes or until doubled in bulk. Brush loaves gently with melted butter. Sprinkle with remaining ¼ cup shredded cheese.

Bake at 375° for 20 to 22 minutes or until golden. Remove from pan immediately. Cool on wire racks.
Yield: 2 loaves.

One-Hour Wild Rice-Parmesan Rolls

This quick-rise method gives you delicious dinner rolls in an hour. Serve them with Steak and Two Potato Soup (page 131).

3½ to 4 cups bread flour, divided
2   (¼-ounce) envelopes rapid-rise yeast
2   tablespoons sugar
2   teaspoons garlic salt
1   cup milk
3   tablespoons butter or margarine
1   large egg
¾   cup cooked wild rice, cooled
1½ cups (6 ounces) freshly grated Parmesan cheese, divided
3   tablespoons butter or margarine, melted

Combine 1½ cups flour, yeast, sugar, and garlic salt in a large mixing bowl; stir well.

Combine milk and 3 tablespoons butter in a small saucepan; cook over medium heat 2 to 3 minutes or until butter melts. Cool to 100° to 110°.

Gradually add milk mixture to flour mixture, beating well at medium speed with an electric mixer. Add egg, beating well. Add rice and ½ cup Parmesan cheese; beat well. Using a wooden spoon, gradually stir in enough remaining flour to make a soft dough.

Turn dough out onto a lightly floured surface, and knead until smooth and elastic (about 6 to 8 minutes). Shape dough into a ball; place in a well-greased bowl, turning to grease top. Cover.

Turn oven to 200° for 1 minute; turn oven off. Place dough in oven; let rise 15 minutes.

Punch dough down; turn out onto a lightly floured surface, and knead lightly 4 or 5 times. Divide dough into 16 pieces; shape into balls. Dip tops of balls into melted butter; dip into remaining 1 cup Parmesan cheese. Arrange balls on a greased 15" x 10" jellyroll pan; let rest 5 minutes.

Bake at 375° for 18 minutes or until lightly browned.
Yield: 16 rolls.

GREAT COFFEE CAKES

'Tis the season for baking, and nothing ushers in the holidays quite like a homemade coffee cake. Peek at our selection of baked goods, including streusel tops and sticky buns.

Buttered Rum
Coffee Cake

BUTTERED RUM COFFEE CAKE

Inside these gooey breakfast rolls you get the crunch of crushed butterscotch candies and a little taste of dark rum. More rum's in the topping.

1   (16-ounce) package hot roll mix
⅔   cup warm milk (100° to 110°)
2   large eggs, lightly beaten
1   teaspoon vanilla extract
½   cup firmly packed light brown sugar
¼   cup crushed butterscotch candies (about 9 candies)
3   tablespoons butter or margarine, softened
2   tablespoons dark rum
1   teaspoon ground cinnamon
Buttered Rum Topping

   Remove yeast packet from roll mix. Sprinkle yeast over warm milk in a large mixing bowl; let stand 5 minutes. Stir in eggs and vanilla. Add 1 cup hot roll mix; beat 2 minutes at medium speed with an electric mixer. Stir in remaining hot roll mix with a wooden spoon until thoroughly blended (dough will be soft). Cover and let rise in a warm place (85°), free from drafts, 1 hour or until doubled in bulk.
   Punch dough down; let rest 5 minutes, and turn out onto a lightly floured surface. Roll into a 12" x 16" rectangle.
   Combine brown sugar and next 4 ingredients; stir until smooth. Spread rum mixture over dough, leaving a 1" margin. Roll up dough, jellyroll fashion, starting at long side; pinch seam to seal. Cut into 16 (1") slices.
   Spread Buttered Rum Topping into bottom of a well-greased 10" tube pan. Stand 10 dough slices against outer edge of pan. Stand remaining 6 slices against center tube of pan. Cover and let rise in a warm place, free from drafts, 50 minutes or until doubled in bulk.
   Bake at 375° for 20 minutes or until lightly browned. Cool 2 minutes in pan; invert onto a serving platter. Drizzle any remaining glaze over cake. **Yield:** 1 (10") coffee cake.

BUTTERED RUM TOPPING

½   cup firmly packed light brown sugar
¼   cup butter or margarine, softened
2   tablespoons dark rum
½   cup chopped walnuts

   Combine brown sugar, butter, and rum. Stir in walnuts. **Yield:** about ¾ cup.

PUMPKIN-PISTACHIO BREAKFAST BREAD

The Pistachio Topping adds a crunchy dimension to this holiday quick bread.

1½   cups butter or margarine, softened
1½   cups sugar
3   large eggs
3   cups all-purpose flour
2   teaspoons baking powder
½   teaspoon baking soda
¾   teaspoon salt
1   teaspoon ground cinnamon
½   teaspoon ground ginger
¼   teaspoon ground cloves
1½   cups canned mashed pumpkin
1   cup raisins
1½   teaspoons vanilla extract
Pistachio Topping
½   (3-ounce) package cream cheese, softened
1   cup sifted powdered sugar
2   tablespoons milk

   Beat butter at medium speed with an electric mixer until creamy; gradually add 1½ cups sugar, beating well. Add eggs, 1 at a time, beating until blended after each addition.
   Combine flour and next 6 ingredients in a large bowl; add to butter mixture alternately with pumpkin, beginning and ending with flour mixture. Stir in raisins and vanilla.
   Spread batter into a greased and floured 13" x 9" pan; sprinkle with Pistachio Topping. Bake at 350° for 45 to 50 minutes or until a wooden pick inserted in center comes out clean. Cool on a wire rack.
   Beat cream cheese, powdered sugar, and milk in a small bowl until smooth, using a wire whisk. Using whisk, drizzle cream cheese mixture over cake. **Yield:** 12 servings.

PISTACHIO TOPPING

⅔   cup unsalted pistachio nuts
⅓   cup firmly packed light brown sugar
¼   cup all-purpose flour
½   teaspoon ground cinnamon
¼   teaspoon ground ginger
⅛   teaspoon ground cloves
2   tablespoons butter or margarine, cut into pieces

   Process first 6 ingredients in a food processor until nuts are coarsely chopped. Add butter to processor; pulse until mixture is crumbly. Set aside. **Yield:** 1 cup.

Coffee Lovers'
Coffee Cake

COFFEE LOVERS' COFFEE CAKE

A buttery coffee crumb mixture makes a shortbreadlike crust for this easy snack cake.

2   cups all-purpose flour
2   teaspoons instant coffee granules
2   cups firmly packed light brown sugar
1   teaspoon ground cinnamon
½   teaspoon salt
½   cup butter or margarine, cut into pieces
1   (8-ounce) carton sour cream
1   teaspoon baking soda
1   large egg, lightly beaten
¾   cup chopped pecans or walnuts

Combine flour and coffee granules in a large bowl. Add brown sugar, cinnamon, and salt; stir well. Cut in butter with a pastry blender until crumbly. Press half of crumb mixture into a greased 9" square pan; set aside.

Combine sour cream and baking soda, stirring well. Add to remaining crumb mixture, stirring just until dry ingredients are moistened. Add egg, stirring gently to combine. Pour sour cream mixture over crumb crust in pan; sprinkle with pecans. Bake at 350° for 45 minutes. **Yield:** 1 (9") coffee cake.

STICKY BUN COFFEE CAKE

Dried fruits, sugar, and spices cook into a thick, syrupy topping for this breakfast bread that starts with canned biscuits. You'll want to lick the pan after baking.

1   cup firmly packed light brown sugar
½   cup dried apricots, finely chopped
½   cup dried figs, finely chopped
½   cup whole pitted dates, finely chopped
½   cup orange juice
¼   cup water
1   (3") cinnamon stick
½   cup chopped pecans, toasted
½   teaspoon vanilla extract
1   cup sugar
2   tablespoons ground cinnamon
2   (16.3-ounce) cans refrigerated buttermilk biscuits
½   cup butter or margarine, melted

Stir together first 7 ingredients in a large saucepan. Bring to a boil; reduce heat and simmer, uncovered, 25 minutes or until fruit is tender and mixture is thick and syrupy. Discard cinnamon stick. Stir in pecans and vanilla. Pour mixture into a greased 12-cup Bundt pan; set aside.

Combine sugar and ground cinnamon in a shallow dish. Cut biscuits into fourths, using kitchen shears. Dip biscuit pieces in melted butter; dredge in sugar mixture. Layer biscuits loosely over fruit mixture in pan.

Bake at 350° for 35 to 40 minutes. Carefully invert cake onto a platter. Drizzle any remaining glaze over cake. Serve warm. **Yield:** 1 (10") coffee cake.

WHITE CHOCOLATE-MACADAMIA COFFEE CAKE

A sugary macadamia streusel and a drizzle of white chocolate distinguish this tender, irresistible coffee cake.

½   cup butter or margarine, softened
¼   cup shortening
1   cup sugar
2   large eggs
2¼ cups all-purpose flour, divided
1   tablespoon baking powder
½   teaspoon salt
1   cup milk
1   teaspoon vanilla extract
1   teaspoon almond extract
1   cup finely chopped macadamia nuts, divided
1   cup (6 ounces) white chocolate morsels, divided
½   cup firmly packed light brown sugar
½   cup uncooked regular oats
¼   cup butter or margarine, softened

Beat ½ cup butter and shortening at medium speed with an electric mixer until creamy; gradually add 1 cup sugar, beating well. Add eggs, 1 at a time, beating until blended after each addition.

Combine 2 cups flour, baking powder, and salt; add to butter mixture alternately with milk, beginning and ending with flour mixture. Beat at low speed until blended after each addition. Stir in flavorings, ½ cup macadamia nuts, and ½ cup white chocolate morsels. Pour batter into a greased and floured 9" x 3" springform pan.

Combine remaining ½ cup macadamia nuts, brown sugar, oats, ¼ cup butter, and remaining ¼ cup flour; stir until crumbly. Sprinkle oat mixture over batter.

Bake at 350° for 50 to 60 minutes or until a wooden pick inserted in center comes out clean. Cool in pan on a wire rack 10 minutes. Run a knife between cake and pan to release cake; remove sides of pan, and cool on wire rack.

Place remaining ½ cup white chocolate morsels in a small heavy-duty zip-top plastic bag. Seal bag. Dip bag in very hot water 2 to 3 minutes or until morsels melt. Remove bag from water; snip a tiny hole in 1 corner of bag. Drizzle white chocolate over coffee cake. **Yield:** 1 (9") coffee cake.

White Chocolate-
Macadamia Coffee Cake

CHEDDAR-APPLE VANOCKA

This version of vanocka, a traditional braided Czech Christmas bread, is laced with golden saffron threads, but it's the apple and cheese filling that'll make you cut that second slice.

8   to 9 cups all-purpose flour, divided
¾   cup sugar
2   teaspoons salt
1   (¼-ounce) envelope active dry yeast
2½   cups hot water (120° to 130°)
¼   teaspoon saffron threads, crumbled
½   cup shortening
1   large egg, beaten
Cheddar-Apple Filling
1   large egg, lightly beaten
½   cup apple jelly, melted
¼   cup powdered sugar

Combine 3 cups all-purpose flour, sugar, salt, and yeast in a large mixing bowl; stir well. Combine water, saffron, and shortening; heat in a saucepan until mixture reaches 120° (shortening does not need to melt completely).

Add liquid mixture to flour mixture, beating well at medium speed with a heavy-duty mixer using the paddle attachment. Add 1 egg and 1 cup flour. Beat at low speed 1 minute; then beat at medium-high speed for 3 minutes. Stir in enough remaining flour to make a soft dough.

Turn dough out onto a lightly floured surface, and knead until smooth and elastic (about 10 minutes). Shape dough into a ball; place in a well-greased bowl, turning to grease top. Cover and let rise in a warm place (85°), free from drafts, 45 minutes or until doubled in bulk.

Punch dough down, and divide in half. Set half of dough aside. (Cover to prevent drying.)

Divide remaining half of dough into 4 equal portions. Combine 3 portions; knead 2 or 3 times on a lightly floured surface. Cover and set aside remaining portion of dough. Roll larger portion into a 13" x 10" rectangle; transfer to a lightly greased baking sheet.

Spoon half of Cheddar-Apple filling in a 4" wide strip down the center of dough, leaving 3" on each side. With a sharp knife, slit dough at 1" intervals along each side of filling. Fold strips over filling, alternating from side to side, tucking ends in.

Divide reserved smaller portion of dough into thirds. Shape each third into a 14" rope; pinch ends together at one end to seal. Braid ropes; pinch loose ends to seal.

Brush top of apple-filled braid lightly with 1 beaten egg; place smaller braid across top of larger braid. Brush smaller braid with egg. Tuck ends of smaller braid under bottom edge of larger braid, pinching to seal. (Place a wooden pick through braids at both ends to prevent separation during rising and baking.)

Repeat rolling, cutting, filling, and braiding procedures with remaining half of dough and filling. Cover and let loaves rise in a warm place, free from drafts, 45 minutes or until doubled in bulk.

Bake at 350° for 25 to 30 minutes or until lightly browned. Transfer to a wire rack; remove wooden picks, and cool. Brush with melted apple jelly; cool. Sift powdered sugar over loaves before serving. **Yield:** 2 loaves.

CHEDDAR-APPLE FILLING

¼   cup butter or margarine
1   cup firmly packed light brown sugar
3½   cups peeled, chopped Granny Smith apple (about 3 apples)
2   tablespoons cornstarch
2   tablespoons water
1½   cups (6 ounces) shredded sharp Cheddar cheese

Melt butter and brown sugar in a large saucepan over medium heat, stirring often. Add chopped apple; bring to a boil. Reduce heat to medium-low, and simmer, uncovered, 20 minutes or until apple is soft. Stir together cornstarch and water. Stir cornstarch mixture into apple filling; cook 1 minute or until mixture thickens. Remove from heat. Cool completely. Stir in cheese. **Yield:** about 2 cups.

Cheddar-Apple
Vanocka

Cranberry-Ginger
Crumble Cake

CRANBERRY-GINGER CRUMBLE CAKE

A ribbon of cranberry filling and a yummy candied ginger topping invite you to take a forkful of this coffee cake.

2   cups fresh or frozen cranberries
1½ cups sugar
1   tablespoon cornstarch
1½ teaspoons grated lemon rind
¾   cup water
¾   cup all-purpose flour
¼   cup sugar
¼   cup cold butter or margarine, cut into pieces
1   (2.7-ounce) jar crystallized ginger, finely chopped
     (½ cup)
1   (8-ounce) package cream cheese, softened
½   cup butter or margarine, softened
¾   cup sugar
2   large eggs
2   cups all-purpose flour
1½ teaspoons baking powder
½   teaspoon baking soda
½   teaspoon salt
¼   cup milk
½   teaspoon vanilla extract

   Stir together first 4 ingredients in a saucepan; stir in water. Bring to a boil; reduce heat, and simmer, uncovered, 25 minutes or until cranberry skins pop and mixture is thickened. Remove from heat; set aside to cool.
   Combine ¾ cup flour, ¼ cup sugar, and ¼ cup butter with a pastry blender until crumbly. Stir in ginger; set aside.
   Beat cream cheese and ½ cup butter at medium speed with an electric mixer until creamy; gradually add ¾ cup sugar, beating well. Add eggs, 1 at a time, beating until blended after each addition.
   Combine 2 cups flour and next 3 ingredients; add to cream cheese mixture alternately with milk, beginning and ending with flour mixture. Beat at low speed until blended after each addition. Stir in vanilla. Spoon half of batter into a greased 13" x 9" pan. Spread reserved cranberry mixture over batter. Drop remaining batter by rounded tablespoonfuls over cranberry mixture. Sprinkle with ginger topping.
   Bake at 350° for 32 to 35 minutes or until a wooden pick inserted in center comes out clean. Cool in pan on a wire rack. **Yield:** 12 servings.

DOUBLE MACAROON COFFEE CAKE

If you like macaroon cookies, you'll love this decadent coffee cake replete with a coconut-almond-flavored filling and an almond streusel top.

¾ cup butter or margarine, softened
1 cup sugar
2 large eggs
2 cups all-purpose flour
2½ teaspoons baking powder
½ teaspoon baking soda
½ teaspoon salt, divided
1 cup sour cream
½ teaspoon coconut extract
¾ teaspoon almond extract, divided
2 cups flaked coconut
⅔ cup sweetened condensed milk
⅓ cup all-purpose flour
¼ cup sugar
½ cup slivered almonds, chopped
¼ cup butter or margarine, cut into pieces

Beat ¾ cup butter at medium speed with an electric mixer until creamy. Gradually add 1 cup sugar, beating well. Add eggs, 1 at a time, beating until blended after each addition.

Combine 2 cups flour, baking powder, baking soda, and ¼ teaspoon salt; add to butter mixture alternately with sour cream, beginning and ending with flour mixture. Beat at low speed until blended after each addition. Stir in coconut extract and ½ teaspoon almond extract.

Spoon half of batter into a greased 9" square pan. Combine flaked coconut, sweetened condensed milk, remaining ¼ teaspoon salt, and remaining ¼ teaspoon almond extract; stir well. Spread over batter in pan. Spread remaining batter over coconut mixture.

Combine ⅓ cup flour, ¼ cup sugar, and almonds. Cut ¼ cup butter into flour mixture with a pastry blender until crumbly. Sprinkle mixture over batter. Bake at 350° for 30 to 35 minutes or until a wooden pick inserted in center comes out clean. Cool in pan on a wire rack. **Yield:** 9 servings.

EGGNOG COFFEE CAKE

Eggnog makes a delicious addition to this quick coffee cake. Canned eggnog is a fine option if you can't find fresh.

2 tablespoons fine, dry breadcrumbs
2 cups all-purpose flour
1 cup sugar
½ teaspoon salt
¾ cup butter, cut into pieces
2 teaspoons baking powder
¾ teaspoon freshly grated nutmeg, divided
1 cup refrigerated eggnog
1 large egg, lightly beaten
3 tablespoons bourbon
1 teaspoon vanilla extract
⅓ cup firmly packed dark brown sugar
½ teaspoon ground cinnamon

Grease a 9" cakepan; sprinkle with breadcrumbs, and tap out excess. Set pan aside.

Combine flour, sugar, salt, and butter with a pastry blender until crumbly. Remove 1 cup crumb mixture; set aside. Stir baking powder and ¼ teaspoon nutmeg into remaining crumb mixture.

Stir together eggnog, egg, bourbon, and vanilla. Add eggnog mixture to crumb mixture; beat at medium-high speed with an electric mixer 2 minutes. Pour batter into prepared pan.

Combine brown sugar, cinnamon, and remaining ½ teaspoon nutmeg to reserved 1 cup crumb mixture; sprinkle over batter. Bake at 375° for 45 to 50 minutes or until a wooden pick inserted in center comes out clean. Serve warm or at room temperature. **Yield:** 1 (9") coffee cake.

WINTER-FRESH RECIPES

Usher in the season with fresh produce. Weave winter fruits and vegetables into your first holiday menu, or arrange them on your table.

PASTRY PILLOWS WITH CREAMED ENDIVE

A flavorful blend of leeks and endive fills these crispy puffs. Serve them in pairs as the start of a meal or as a side dish with beef or chicken.

1½ cups sliced leeks (about 2 leeks)
2 tablespoons butter or margarine, melted
1¼ pounds Belgian endive, thinly sliced (about 6 heads)
¾ cup chicken broth
3 tablespoons fresh lemon juice
1 teaspoon salt
¼ teaspoon pepper
¾ cup whipping cream
1 tablespoon butter or margarine
1 tablespoon chopped fresh chives
½ (17¼-ounce) package frozen puff pastry, thawed
Garnish: fresh chives

Sauté leeks in 2 tablespoons melted butter in a large skillet or sauté pan over medium heat 5 minutes. Add endive and next 4 ingredients. Simmer 3 minutes; add whipping cream. Simmer, uncovered, over medium-high heat 10 minutes or until cream is reduced by half. Stir in 1 tablespoon butter and 1 tablespoon chopped chives.

Meanwhile, cut puff pastry sheet into thirds along fold lines. Cut each strip into 5 (2"-wide) rectangles; place on an ungreased baking sheet. Bake at 425° for 15 minutes or until puffed and golden; cool 3 minutes.

To serve, gently cut off top of each puff pastry, and spoon about 3 tablespoons endive filling onto puff pastry bottom; replace top. Garnish, if desired. Serve immediately. **Yield:** 15 puff pastries.

Pastry Pillows with
Creamed Endive

BUTTERNUT SQUASH RAVIOLI WITH SAGE BUTTER SAUCE

Butternut squash, crushed gingersnaps, and aged Parmesan become an incredible filling for tender ravioli that make an elegant seated appetizer.

½ cup crushed gingersnaps (about 8 cookies)
2 tablespoons milk
1 (2-pound) butternut squash
1 cup (4 ounces) freshly grated Parmigiano-Reggiano cheese, divided
2 tablespoons butter, softened
½ teaspoon salt
1 (12-ounce) package won ton wrappers
Sage Butter Sauce
Freshly ground pepper

Stir together gingersnaps and milk in a medium bowl. Let stand until cookies are softened (about 10 minutes).

Cut squash in half lengthwise; remove seeds. Line a baking sheet with aluminum foil. Coat foil with cooking spray. Place squash, cut side down, on foil. Bake, uncovered, at 400° for 30 to 40 minutes or until tender. Scoop out pulp; mash. Discard shell. Measure 1¾ cups pulp; reserve any remaining pulp for another use.

Stir 1¾ cups squash pulp, ½ cup cheese, butter, and salt into softened gingersnaps. Working with 6 won ton wrappers at a time (keeping remaining wrappers covered), spoon about 1 tablespoon squash filling into center of each wrapper. Moisten edges of each wrapper with water; bring 2 opposite corners together. Press edges together with a fork to seal, forming a triangle. Cover ravioli with a damp towel to keep them from drying.

Bring 2 quarts water to a boil in a large saucepan. Cook ravioli, 6 at a time, uncovered, 1 to 2 minutes. Quickly remove from water with a slotted spoon. Keep warm. Place 6 ravioli in each serving bowl. Top each with 1 tablespoon Sage Butter Sauce. Sprinkle evenly with remaining ½ cup cheese and pepper. **Yield:** 8 servings.

SAGE BUTTER SAUCE

½ cup butter
⅓ cup fresh sage leaves, cut into thin strips

Melt butter in a small saucepan over medium heat; cook, stirring constantly, 3 minutes or until golden. Stir in sage, and cook 15 seconds. (Do not brown.) Remove from heat. **Yield:** ½ cup.

Butternut Squash Ravioli with Sage Butter Sauce

LEMON-BAKED CAULIFLOWER

For a splash of Christmas color, stir diced pimiento into the buttery topping for this cauliflower.

⅓ cup finely chopped shallots
¼ cup butter or margarine, softened
¼ cup finely chopped fresh parsley
2 garlic cloves, minced
1 tablespoon grated lemon rind
1 teaspoon salt
¼ teaspoon pepper
⅛ teaspoon ground nutmeg
1 large cauliflower, cored

Stir together first 8 ingredients.

Place cauliflower on a large sheet of heavy-duty aluminum foil; spread butter mixture over cauliflower. Bring sides of foil to top; seal edges. Place on a baking sheet. Bake at 375° for 1 hour or until tender. **Yield:** 6 servings.

LEMON-BRAISED BRUSSELS SPROUTS

Instead of grating lemon rind, we used a citrus zester for slender strands of zest. Remember to remove the zest from lemons before squeezing them for fresh juice.

1½ pounds fresh brussels sprouts
2   tablespoons butter or margarine
½   cup fresh lemon juice
½   cup water
2   tablespoons brown sugar
½   teaspoon salt
2   teaspoons lemon zest
⅛   teaspoon freshly ground pepper

Wash brussels sprouts; remove discolored leaves. Trim ends, and cut sprouts in half lengthwise; set aside.

Melt butter in a large skillet; add lemon juice, water, brown sugar, and salt. Bring to a boil. Add brussels sprouts; cover, reduce heat, and simmer 15 minutes or until sprouts are tender. Uncover, increase heat to high, and cook 4 minutes or until most of liquid evaporates. Remove from heat. Stir in lemon zest and freshly ground pepper. **Yield:** 4 servings.

ACORN SQUASH SOUP

The delicate flavor of winter squash is enhanced by cinnamon and other spices in this creamy soup fit for the holiday table.

2   acorn squash, halved and seeded
1   large yellow onion, chopped
1   tablespoon butter or margarine, melted
2   tablespoons light brown sugar
3   cups chicken broth
1   teaspoon salt
1   teaspoon ground cinnamon
1   teaspoon ground coriander
¼   teaspoon pepper
½   cup whipping cream

Cut squash in half crosswise; remove seeds. Place squash, cut side down, in a greased shallow baking dish. Bake at 400° for 45 minutes or until tender; cool. Scoop out pulp, discarding shells.

Sauté onion in butter in a Dutch oven over medium-high heat 7 to 8 minutes or until lightly browned. Add brown sugar; cook 2 minutes, stirring often. Add squash pulp; cook 5 minutes, stirring often. Add broth and next

4 ingredients. Cover, reduce heat to medium-low, and simmer 5 minutes. Remove from heat; cool slightly.

Process soup, in batches, in a food processor or blender until smooth. Return soup to Dutch oven; simmer 5 minutes. Drizzle each serving with a little whipping cream. **Yield:** 7½ cups.

PARSNIP FRITTERS

Pop these crisp little fritters in your mouth for a mild taste of parsnip with a hint of nutmeg. Serve them as a side dish or appetizer.

2   pounds parsnips, scraped and cut into 1½" pieces
⅓   cup minced purple onion
1   large egg
1   egg yolk
1   tablespoon butter or margarine, melted
1   teaspoon ground mustard
1   teaspoon salt
½   teaspoon pepper
¼   teaspoon grated nutmeg
⅓   cup all-purpose flour
Peanut oil
Salt

Cook parsnips in boiling water to cover in a large saucepan 20 to 25 minutes or until very tender. Drain well.

Process parsnips and next 8 ingredients in a food processor until pureed. Transfer mixture to a bowl; stir in flour.

Pour oil to depth of 2" into a large heavy skillet; heat to 375° over medium-high heat. Using 2 teaspoons, shape about 1½ tablespoons parsnip mixture into a fritter by rounding mixture between edges of spoons. Drop fritters into hot oil, 6 at a time, and cook 2 to 3 minutes or until golden, turning once. Drain on paper towels.

Transfer fritters to a baking sheet; sprinkle lightly with salt, and keep warm in a 300° oven. Repeat with remaining mixture. Serve hot. **Yield:** 6 servings.

POTATO, LEEK, AND FENNEL GRATIN

You won't be disappointed when you spoon into this rustic gratin. It sports a crusty cheese top and tender potatoes swimming in a rich-as-they-come cheese sauce.

2   large fennel bulbs
2   leeks
2   tablespoons butter or margarine, melted
¾   teaspoon salt
1   teaspoon chopped fresh thyme
2   pounds baking potatoes, peeled and thinly sliced
2   tablespoons all-purpose flour
½   teaspoon salt
¾   cup whipping cream
⅔   cup milk
3   cups (12 ounces) shredded Gruyère cheese, divided
2   teaspoons chopped fresh thyme, divided
¼   teaspoon freshly ground pepper

Rinse fennel thoroughly. Trim stalks to within 1" of bulbs. Discard hard outside stalks; reserve fennel tops for another use. Cut a slice off bottom of bulbs. Cut out core from bottom of bulbs. Starting at 1 side, cut bulbs lengthwise into ¼"-thick slices. Set aside.

Remove root, tough outer leaves, and tops from leeks, leaving 1" of dark leaves. Wash leeks thoroughly; cut into ¼"-thick slices.

Sauté fennel and leeks in melted butter in a large skillet over medium-high heat 5 minutes. Add ¾ teaspoon salt and 1 teaspoon thyme; cover, reduce heat, and simmer, stirring occasionally, 10 minutes. Set aside.

Combine potato, flour, and ½ teaspoon salt in a large zip-top plastic bag. Seal; toss to coat well. Arrange half of potato in a buttered gratin dish or 13" x 9" baking dish.

Combine whipping cream and milk; pour half of cream mixture over potato. Sprinkle 1½ cups cheese and 1 teaspoon thyme over potato. Spoon sautéed fennel and leek over cheese, and top with remaining potato. Pour remaining cream mixture over potato, and sprinkle with remaining 1½ cups cheese, 1 teaspoon thyme, and pepper.

Bake, covered, at 400° for 45 minutes. Uncover and bake 15 more minutes or until browned. Let stand 10 minutes before serving. **Yield:** 8 to 10 servings.

Potato, Leek, and Fennel Gratin

Grapefruit-Rosemary
Daiquiris

GRAPEFRUIT-ROSEMARY DAIQUIRIS

You won't believe how good grapefruit and rosemary taste together in this slushy daiquiri. Lining the glasses with coarse sugar really adds something to each sip.

3   cups freshly squeezed ruby red grapefruit juice (about
    7 grapefruit)
1½ cups water
⅔ cup sugar
2   large sprigs fresh rosemary
⅓ cup vodka
1½ teaspoons finely chopped fresh rosemary
Sparkling white sugar (optional)
Garnish: fresh rosemary sprigs

Pour 2½ cups grapefruit juice into 2 ice cube trays; freeze until firm. Cover and chill remaining juice.

Stir together water, sugar, and 2 rosemary sprigs in a saucepan; bring to a boil. Cover, reduce heat, and simmer 10 minutes. Remove from heat; discard rosemary. Cool syrup; chill.

Process frozen juice cubes, remaining ½ cup grapefruit juice, rosemary syrup, vodka, and chopped rosemary in a 5-cup blender for 10 seconds or until slushy. Serve in sugar-rimmed glasses, and garnish, if desired. **Yield:** 5 cups.

GINGERED AMBROSIA

Fresh ginger and mint bring new life to a holiday favorite.

6 large navel oranges
2½ tablespoons fresh lime juice (about 1 lime)
1½ tablespoons grated fresh ginger
1 peeled and cored fresh pineapple, cut into bite-size pieces (see Note below)
⅔ cup flaked coconut
¼ cup fresh mint leaves, cut into thin strips
Garnishes: fresh mint sprigs, lime slices

Peel and section oranges over a bowl, reserving any juice. Squeeze membranes to catch any remaining juice. Set orange sections aside.

Add lime juice and ginger to orange juice in bowl. Add orange sections, pineapple, coconut, and ¼ cup mint; toss gently. Cover and chill until ready to serve. Garnish, if desired. **Yield:** 6 to 8 servings.

Note: *You can buy a peeled and cored fresh pineapple in the produce section of the grocery store.*

Gingered Ambrosia

ROASTED PEARS WITH GORGONZOLA CREAM

Here's a not-so-sweet fruit and cheese dessert.

3 large ripe Bosc pears, peeled and halved
2 tablespoons butter or margarine, melted
1 (3-ounce) package cream cheese, softened
3 ounces Gorgonzola cheese, softened
2 tablespoons whipping cream
¼ cup walnuts, finely chopped
Ground cinnamon
Honey

Scoop out core from each pear half with a melon baller, leaving at least a 1"-thick shell. Slice about ¼" from rounded sides to make pear halves sit flat, if necessary. Brush cut side of each pear half with melted butter, and place, cored side up, on a greased baking sheet. Bake, uncovered, at 450° for 15 minutes.

Process cheeses and whipping cream in a food processor until creamy. Spoon mixture into center of each warm pear half. Broil pears 3" from heat 1 to 2 minutes or until lightly browned. Place pears on serving plates. Sprinkle with walnuts. Sprinkle very lightly with cinnamon, and drizzle with honey. Serve warm. **Yield:** 6 servings.

CRANBERRY-PEAR CRISP

5 firm ripe Bosc pears, peeled and cut into 1" chunks
¾ cup dried cranberries
¼ cup honey
¼ cup sugar
1 tablespoon lemon juice
1½ cups uncooked regular oats
¾ cup firmly packed light brown sugar
½ cup all-purpose flour
2 teaspoons ground cinnamon
½ teaspoon salt
½ cup butter or margarine, cut into pieces and softened

Stir together first 5 ingredients; spoon pear filling into a greased 8" square baking dish.

Combine oats and next 4 ingredients; add butter, stirring well. Pinch topping into large crumbs. Sprinkle topping over pear filling. Bake, uncovered, at 375° for 40 minutes or until pears are tender and topping is golden. Let stand 15 minutes. Serve warm with ice cream or unsweetened whipped cream. **Yield:** 6 servings.

Cranberry-Pear
Crisp

CHRISTMAS CHOCOLATES

*Craving chocolate this holiday season? Here's a baker's dozen
delectable desserts to delight you and your guests.*

(Clockwise from front) German
Chocolate Roulage, Double-Nut
Drenched Chocolate Cake,
Espresso Crunch Cups, Chocolate-
Peanut Butter Biscotti

DOUBLE-NUT DRENCHED CHOCOLATE CAKE

Hazelnut fans will enjoy this triple-decker chocolate-topped cake. Chocolate and vanilla layers are soaked with Frangelico and then iced with a divine fudgy topping.

¾ cup butter, softened
2 cups firmly packed light brown sugar
2 large eggs
¾ cup water
¼ cup white vinegar
2 cups all-purpose flour
1 teaspoon baking soda
¼ teaspoon salt
1 cup finely chopped hazelnuts, toasted
1 tablespoon vanilla extract
¼ cup cocoa
½ cup Frangelico
Chocolate Topping
Garnishes: pecan halves, hazelnuts

Grease and flour 3 (8") round cakepans; line bottoms with wax paper. Grease paper and sides of pans. Set aside.

Beat butter at medium speed with an electric mixer until creamy. Gradually add brown sugar, beating at high speed until light and fluffy. Add eggs, 1 at a time, beating until blended after each addition.

Stir together water and vinegar. Combine flour, baking soda, and salt; add to butter mixture alternately with water mixture, beginning and ending with flour mixture. Beat at low speed until blended after each addition. Stir in chopped nuts and vanilla. Pour one-third of batter into each of 2 prepared pans. Fold cocoa into remaining batter; pour chocolate batter into third pan.

Bake at 350° for 18 to 20 minutes or until cake layers spring back when lightly touched. Cool in pans on wire racks 10 minutes; remove from pans. Peel off wax paper immediately after inverting. Cool on wire racks. Drizzle Frangelico evenly over cake layers.

Spread one-third of Chocolate Topping over 1 white cake layer (do not frost sides). Top with chocolate cake layer; spread one-third of Chocolate Topping over chocolate cake layer (do not frost sides). Top with remaining white cake layer and Chocolate Topping (do not frost sides). Garnish, if desired. Allow cake to set several hours before slicing. **Yield:** 1 (3-layer) cake.

CHOCOLATE TOPPING

3 (4-ounce) bars sweet baking chocolate, chopped
1 cup butter
¾ cup chopped pecans
1 teaspoon vanilla extract

Melt chocolate and butter in a heavy saucepan over medium-low heat; cool 10 minutes. Stir in pecans and vanilla; cool until spreading consistency. **Yield:** 3 cups.

ESPRESSO CRUNCH CUPS

Serve these petite chocolate cups chilled. Each has a little espresso bean crunch in the center.

¼ cup butter or margarine, softened
2¼ cups sifted powdered sugar
¾ cup crushed chocolate-covered espresso beans (4 ounces)
3 tablespoons Kahlúa
⅛ teaspoon salt
3 cups (18 ounces) milk chocolate morsels
3 tablespoons shortening
48 (1½") paper candy cups

Beat butter at medium speed with an electric mixer about 2 minutes or until creamy. Gradually add powdered sugar, beating until smooth. Stir in espresso beans, Kahlúa, and salt. Cover and chill 1 hour or until firm. Shape mixture by teaspoonfuls into balls, and flatten slightly.

Melt chocolate morsels and shortening in a small saucepan over low heat, stirring until smooth. Spoon ½ teaspoon melted chocolate into 48 paper-lined miniature (1¾") muffin pans, turning pans to coat bottoms evenly. Place 1 Kahlúa ball in each cup; spoon remaining melted chocolate over Kahlúa balls, covering them completely. Cover and chill chocolate cups until firm. Store in an airtight container in refrigerator. **Yield:** 4 dozen.

CHOCOLATE-PEANUT BUTTER BISCOTTI

Peanut butter pays a compliment to chocolate in these crunchy cookies.

⅓   cup creamy peanut butter
¾   cup sugar
2   large eggs
1½ cups all-purpose flour
⅓   cup cocoa
¾   teaspoon baking soda
¼   teaspoon salt
½   cup finely chopped peanuts (we tested with cocktail
      peanuts)
1½ cups semisweet chocolate mini-morsels, divided
1½ tablespoons creamy peanut butter
1½ tablespoons shortening

Beat ⅓ cup peanut butter and sugar at medium speed with an electric mixer until creamy. Add eggs, beating until blended.

Stir together flour, cocoa, baking soda, and salt; add to peanut butter mixture, beating at low speed until blended. Turn dough out onto a lightly floured surface; knead in peanuts and ½ cup chocolate mini-morsels.

Shape dough into a 13" x 3" log on a lightly greased baking sheet. Bake at 325° for 40 minutes or until firm. Remove to a wire rack to cool (about 20 minutes).

Cut log diagonally into ½"-thick slices with a serrated knife, using a gentle sawing motion; place slices on ungreased baking sheets. Bake at 325° for 7 minutes; turn cookies over, and bake 7 more minutes. Remove to wire racks to cool.

Combine remaining 1 cup chocolate mini-morsels, 1½ tablespoons peanut butter, and shortening in a small saucepan. Cook over low heat until chocolate and peanut butter melt. Dip one end of each biscotti in chocolate mixture. Place biscotti on wax paper until chocolate hardens. **Yield:** 28 cookies.

GERMAN CHOCOLATE ROULAGE

German chocolate cake gets rolled up with the gooey icing on the inside. Then it's covered in a blanket of chocolate and sprinkled with toasted coconut to hint at the flavor inside.

6   large eggs, separated
¾   cup sugar
¼   cup cocoa
1   teaspoon vanilla extract
½   teaspoon cream of tartar
⅛   teaspoon salt
½   cup sifted cake flour
1   to 2 tablespoons cocoa
1   (14-ounce) can sweetened condensed milk
1½ cups flaked coconut, toasted
1   cup chopped pecans, toasted
2   teaspoons vanilla extract
5   tablespoons half-and-half
⅔   cup whipping cream
2   tablespoons light corn syrup
2   (4-ounce) sweet chocolate bars, finely chopped
      (we tested with Baker's)
Garnish: toasted flaked coconut

Chocolate-Peanut
Butter Biscotti

German Chocolate
Roulage

Grease bottom and sides of a 15" x 10" jellyroll pan; line bottom with wax paper. Grease and flour wax paper. Set aside.

Beat egg yolks at high speed with an electric mixer until foamy. Gradually add sugar, beating until thick and pale (about 2 minutes). Gradually add ¼ cup cocoa, beating well. Stir in 1 teaspoon vanilla.

Beat egg whites at high speed until foamy. Add cream of tartar and salt; beat until stiff peaks form. Fold about one-fourth of beaten egg white into yolk mixture; gradually fold in remaining egg white. Sift cake flour over batter, and gently fold until combined.

Spread batter evenly into prepared pan. Bake at 325° for 16 to 17 minutes or until top springs back when lightly touched. Sift 1 to 2 tablespoons cocoa in a 15" x 10" rectangle on a cloth towel. When cake is done, immediately loosen from sides of pan, and turn out onto towel. Peel off wax paper. Starting at narrow end, roll up cake and towel together; cool on a wire rack, seam side down.

Pour sweetened condensed milk into a medium-size heavy saucepan. Cook over medium-low to medium heat, stirring constantly, 20 minutes or until milk turns a light caramel color. Remove from heat, and stir in 1½ cups toasted coconut, chopped pecans, 2 teaspoons vanilla, and half-and-half.

Unroll cake, and remove towel. Spread cake with coconut filling. Carefully reroll cake without towel. Place cake, seam side down, on a wire rack over wax paper.

Stir together whipping cream and corn syrup in a saucepan; bring to a boil over medium heat. Remove from heat, and add chopped chocolate, stirring until smooth. Pour about three-fourths of chocolate mixture over cake, letting excess drip onto wax paper. Let remaining chocolate sit at room temperature until consistency of frosting (about 45 minutes). Spread remaining chocolate mixture onto ends of cake roll. Garnish, if desired. Let cake stand until chocolate is firm. Place cake on a serving platter. **Yield:** 8 to 10 servings.

BLACK-BOTTOM CHOCOLATE CREAM PIE

Thick and rich is the most fitting description for this pie.

1½ (3-ounce) dark chocolate bars, melted (we tested with Ghirardelli; see Note below)
1   baked 9" pastry shell
⅔   cup sugar
⅓   cup cornstarch
3   tablespoons cocoa
⅛   teaspoon salt
4   egg yolks, lightly beaten
2   cups milk
1   cup half-and-half
2   tablespoons butter or margarine
1   (3-ounce) dark chocolate bar, finely chopped
1   teaspoon vanilla extract
1   tablespoon bourbon (optional)
1   cup whipping cream
¼   cup sifted powdered sugar
Garnish: chocolate shavings

Pour melted chocolate into bottom of baked pastry shell, spreading evenly. Chill until chocolate hardens.

Combine ⅔ cup sugar, cornstarch, cocoa, and salt in a heavy saucepan; stir well. Stir together egg yolks, milk, and half-and-half; gradually stir into sugar mixture. Cook over medium heat, stirring constantly, until mixture thickens and boils. Boil 3 minutes, stirring constantly. Remove from heat; stir in butter, chopped chocolate, vanilla, and, if desired, bourbon.

Pour filling into a bowl; place plastic wrap directly over surface of filling, and cool 30 minutes. Pour filling into pastry shell; cover tightly with plastic wrap, and chill at least 6 hours.

Beat whipping cream at medium speed with an electric mixer until foamy; gradually add powdered sugar, beating until soft peaks form. Spread whipped cream over pie. Chill. Garnish, if desired. **Yield:** 1 (9") pie.

Note: *Find dark chocolate bars on the candy aisle at your local grocery store. Other types of chocolate used in this chapter can be found on the baking aisle.*

CHOCOLATE MINT MOUSSE MERINGUES

These crisp, light meringues are the start of a great impromptu dessert, due to their keeping quality. Read more about hard meringues at right.

4   egg whites
½   teaspoon cream of tartar
½   cup sugar
½   cup sifted powdered sugar
½   teaspoon peppermint extract
1½   cups whipping cream
1   (10-ounce) package mint chocolate morsels
Coarsely crushed hard peppermint candies

Line a baking sheet with parchment paper; draw 6 (3½") circles onto paper. Turn paper over to prevent markings from touching meringues; set aside.

Beat egg whites at low speed with an electric mixer until foamy; add cream of tartar. Increase speed to medium; gradually add 2 tablespoons sugar, 1 tablespoon at a time, beating until soft peaks form. Increase speed to high; gradually add remaining 6 tablespoons sugar and ½ cup powdered sugar, 1 tablespoon at a time, beating until stiff peaks form and sugars dissolve (2 to 4 minutes). Fold in peppermint extract.

Immediately spoon meringue into mounds on paper circles. Shape into circles, using the back of a spoon, and mounding the sides at least ½" higher than centers. Bake at 225° for 1 hour and 35 minutes. Turn oven off. Let meringue shells stand in closed oven 8 hours. Peel shells gently from parchment paper. (Store meringue shells in an airtight container up to 2 days before filling.)

Place whipping cream and chocolate morsels in a saucepan. Cook over medium-low heat, stirring constantly, until chocolate melts and mixture is smooth. Remove from heat, and cool completely. Cover and chill at least 8 hours. Beat chocolate mixture at medium-high speed with an electric mixer until thickened and firm.

Spoon mousse evenly into meringue shells; sprinkle with crushed peppermint candies. **Yield:** 6 servings.

Meringue Moxie

Follow the tips below for snow-white, crisp meringues every time.

Want meringues with the most volume?
- Use room temperature eggs. Run eggs (still in the shell) under very warm water 30 seconds; pat dry.
- Beat egg whites in a clean bowl, free of grease; a greasy bowl inhibits fluffy results.
- Use a little cream of tartar; it helps produce a stable meringue that won't deflate. Quickly spoon meringue onto baking sheet, and bake immediately after mixing.

What's the key to crispy?
- Hard meringues have a high sugar content, ¼ cup per egg white. The sugar draws water away from beaten egg whites so that in the oven the meringues become crisp and dry.
- Using powdered sugar makes hard meringues very light.

Can I make them ahead?
- Hard meringues should keep several days when stored in an airtight container. If needed, recrisp them in a 200° oven for 20 to 30 minutes.

WHITE CHOCOLATE-MACADAMIA FUDGE

White chocolate, toasted macadamias, and orange essence bump this fudge up to fabulous.

3   cups (18 ounces) white chocolate morsels
1½   cups miniature marshmallows
1   (14-ounce) can sweetened condensed milk
2   teaspoons grated orange rind
1   teaspoon vanilla extract
⅛   teaspoon salt
1   cup chopped macadamia nuts, toasted

Line a 9" square pan with aluminum foil; lightly grease foil.

Cook first 3 ingredients in a heavy saucepan over medium heat, stirring constantly, 10 to 11 minutes or until smooth. Remove from heat, and stir in orange rind, vanilla, and salt until blended. Stir in nuts.

Pour fudge into prepared pan. Cover and chill at least 4 hours or until firm. Cut fudge into squares, and store in refrigerator. **Yield:** 2 pounds.

White Chocolate-
Macadamia Fudge

CHOCOLATE CHUNK BREAD PUDDING WITH WHITE CHOCOLATE BRANDY SAUCE

Chunks of half-melted chocolate appear in every bite of this sinfully good bread pudding. It gets even better—you serve it in a pool of brandy sauce.

1   (1-pound) loaf day-old French bread
3½ cups milk
1   cup half-and-half
4   large eggs, lightly beaten
1   cup sugar
2   tablespoons butter or margarine, melted
1   tablespoon vanilla extract
⅛   teaspoon salt
2   (4-ounce) bittersweet chocolate bars, chopped
    (we tested with Ghirardelli)
White Chocolate Brandy Sauce

Tear bread into small pieces; place in a large bowl. Add milk and half-and-half; let mixture stand 10 minutes.

Combine eggs, sugar, butter, vanilla, and salt; add to bread, stirring well. Stir in chopped chocolate. Spoon mixture into a lightly greased 13" x 9" pan. Bake, uncovered, at 325° for 55 minutes or until firm and lightly browned. Cut into squares, and serve warm with White Chocolate Brandy Sauce. **Yield:** 9 servings.

WHITE CHOCOLATE BRANDY SAUCE

½   cup sugar
½   cup butter or margarine
½   cup half-and-half
1   (4-ounce) white chocolate bar, chopped (we tested
    with Ghirardelli)
3   tablespoons brandy

Combine first 3 ingredients in a saucepan; bring to a boil over medium heat, stirring until sugar dissolves. Reduce heat, and simmer 5 minutes. Remove from heat; add white chocolate, stirring until chocolate melts. Stir in brandy. Serve warm. **Yield:** 1¾ cups.

Chocolate Chunk Bread Pudding with White Chocolate Brandy Sauce

Congo Bars

CONGO BARS

Everyone likes an easy bar cookie recipe that gets rave reviews. This is one of them.

2   cups firmly packed brown sugar
½   cup butter or margarine, melted
3   large eggs, lightly beaten
1   teaspoon vanilla extract
1½ cups all-purpose flour
1   cup chocolate graham cracker crumbs (about 6 whole crackers)
2   teaspoons baking powder
1   cup salted cashews, chopped
1   (11.5-ounce) package semisweet chocolate chunks or mega morsels

Stir together first 4 ingredients. Combine flour, graham cracker crumbs, and baking powder; add to butter mixture, stirring well. Stir in cashews and chocolate chunks. (Batter will be thick.) Spread batter into a greased 13" x 9" pan. Bake at 350° for 27 minutes. Cool in pan on a wire rack. Cut into bars. **Yield:** 2 dozen.

BROWNIE FREEZER SOUFFLÉS

These soufflés are great for entertaining—you can make them ahead, and then send them from freezer to oven during dinner.

¼   cup butter or margarine
2   (3-ounce) dark chocolate bars (we tested with Ghirardelli; see Note on page 155)
3   tablespoons all-purpose flour
1   cup chocolate milk
¼   teaspoon salt
1   teaspoon vanilla extract
4   large eggs, separated
½   cup sugar
¼   teaspoon cream of tartar
Irish Cream Sauce

Butter bottom and sides of 8 (6-ounce) ramekins; sprinkle with sugar. Set aside.

Melt ¼ cup butter and chocolate in a saucepan over medium-low heat. Add flour; stir until smooth. Cook 1 minute, stirring constantly. Gradually add chocolate milk; cook over medium heat, stirring constantly, until thickened and bubbly. Stir in salt and vanilla. Beat egg yolks and sugar at medium speed with an electric mixer until

thick and pale (about 2 minutes). Gradually stir about one-fourth of hot chocolate mixture into yolk mixture; beat at medium speed until blended. Gradually add remaining hot mixture, beating until blended. Let cool 5 minutes.

Beat egg whites and cream of tartar at high speed until stiff peaks form. Gently fold one-fourth of beaten egg white into chocolate mixture. Gradually fold remaining egg white into chocolate mixture. Carefully spoon mixture into prepared ramekins. Cover and freeze until firm. (See Note below to bake them immediately.)

Remove soufflés from freezer, and let stand 30 minutes. Bake at 350° for 30 minutes or until tops are puffed. Cut a slit in top of each soufflé, and serve immediately with Irish Cream Sauce. **Yield:** 8 servings.

IRISH CREAM SAUCE

¾   cup French vanilla ice cream
3   tablespoons Irish cream liqueur (we tested with Bailey's)
⅓   cup whipping cream, whipped

Place ice cream in a microwave-safe bowl; microwave at HIGH 30 seconds or just until melted. Stir in Irish cream; fold in whipped cream. Store in refrigerator. **Yield:** 1¼ cups.

Note: *You can bake these soufflés immediately without freezing. Bake at 350° for 30 minutes.*

Brownie Freezer
Soufflé

FUDGY PISTACHIO BUNDT CAKE

Sour cream and cocoa flavor this moist cake. It boasts a tender crumb, a thick chocolate glaze, and a festive sprinkling of pistachios.

1   cup cocoa
1   tablespoon instant coffee granules
1½ cups boiling water
1½ cups butter or margarine, softened
2¼ cups sugar
¾   cup firmly packed brown sugar
5   large eggs
1   (8-ounce) container sour cream
1½ teaspoons vanilla extract
2½ cups all-purpose flour
¾   teaspoon baking soda
¼   teaspoon salt
2   cups (12 ounces) semisweet chocolate morsels, divided
¼   cup butter or margarine
3   tablespoons heavy whipping cream
½   cup chopped pistachio nuts, toasted

Combine cocoa, coffee, and boiling water in a bowl, stirring until smooth. Set aside to cool.

Beat 1½ cups butter at medium speed with an electric mixer about 2 minutes or until creamy. Gradually add sugars, beating 5 to 7 minutes. Add eggs, 1 at a time, beating just until yellow disappears.

Add sour cream and vanilla to cooled cocoa mixture. Combine flour, baking soda, and salt; add to butter mixture alternately with cocoa mixture, beginning and ending with flour mixture. Stir in 1 cup chocolate morsels. Pour batter into a heavily greased and floured 10" x 3½" (12-cup) Bundt pan. (Pan will be very full.)

Bake at 350° for 1 hour and 5 minutes or until a long wooden pick inserted in center comes out clean. Cool in pan on a wire rack 15 minutes; remove from pan, and cool on wire rack.

Meanwhile, combine remaining 1 cup chocolate morsels and ¼ cup butter in a small saucepan; cook over low heat until melted. Remove from heat; stir in whipping cream. Let glaze stand 45 minutes.

Place cooled cake on rack over wax paper. Pour chocolate glaze over cake; spoon any excess glaze on wax paper over cake. Sprinkle with pistachios. **Yield:** 1 (10") cake.

Fudgy Pistachio Bundt Cake

Chocolate Scones

PETITE PA

1. Using a c
desired size.
house. Use a
pieces togeth
2. Line the i
(semitranspa
light, if desir
holder in the
Note: Never

BITTERSWEET BRÛLÉE

Crunchy brown sugar shells top these creamy chocolate pudding cups. For company, make these impressive desserts a day ahead.

3	cups whipping cream
6	(1-ounce) squares bittersweet chocolate, coarsely chopped
½	cup sugar

Pinch of salt

1	teaspoon almond extract
1	teaspoon vanilla extract
7	egg yolks, lightly beaten
9	tablespoons brown sugar

Combine first 4 ingredients in a large saucepan. Cook over low heat, stirring constantly, until chocolate melts and mixture is smooth (do not boil). Remove from heat. Stir in flavorings.

Gradually stir about one-fourth of hot whipping cream mixture into beaten egg yolks; add to remaining hot whipping cream mixture, stirring constantly.

Pour custard mixture evenly into 9 (4-ounce) ramekins. Place ramekins in a large roasting pan or 2 (9") pans; add hot water to pan(s) to depth of 1". Bake, covered, at 325° for 40 minutes. Remove ramekins from pan(s); cool slightly on wire racks. Cover and chill up to 24 hours.

Place ramekins on a baking sheet. Sprinkle each with 1 tablespoon brown sugar. Broil 3" from heat just until sugar melts. Cool on wire racks 5 minutes to allow sugar to harden. **Yield:** 9 servings.

CHOCOLATE SCONES

For breakfast or dessert, these brownielike sugar-crusted scones are addicting.

2	cups all-purpose flour
¾	cup sugar
3	tablespoons Dutch process cocoa (we tested with Droste)
2	teaspoons baking powder
½	teaspoon salt
½	cup cold butter, cut into pieces
1	cup whipping cream
2	(1-ounce) squares semisweet chocolate, melted
1	teaspoon vanilla extract
1	tablespoon whipping cream or milk
2	tablespoons turbinado sugar or sugar

Combine first 5 ingredients; cut butter into dry ingredients with a pastry blender until crumbly. Gradually add 1 cup whipping cream, melted chocolate, and vanilla, stirring with a fork just until dry ingredients are moistened. Knead dough in bowl 3 or 4 times to incorporate any flour or cocoa in bottom of bowl.

Pat dough into an 8" circle on a parchment-paper lined or lightly greased baking sheet. Cut into 8 wedges, using a sharp knife. (Do not separate wedges.) Brush with 1 tablespoon whipping cream, and sprinkle with turbinado sugar.

Bake at 425° for 19 to 20 minutes. (Center will be soft; do not overbake.) Serve warm. **Yield:** 8 scones.

PAT
INS

DRESSING U

For each Velvet

Velvet (Ace
color comb
Rubber stan
Pillow stuffi
Large needl

1. Enlarge the
12" from tip to
2. Imprint the
for "A Ring of
rubber stamp d
velvet.
3. With right s
one tip to the c
leaving a 6" ope
4. Turn the pill
stuffing until we
5. With a large
button, and dra
low. Pull the th
Attach a tassel

CARD-IN-A-BOX (PAGE 112)

You will need:
   Rubber stamps and ink pad(s)
   Cardstock paper
   Box or tin container with a removable top
   Glue or double-stick tape
   String, cord, or ribbon
   Assorted beads, charms, and paper cutouts

*See page 172 for rubber stamp ordering information.

1. Stamp two of each desired image or letter onto cardstock, and cut cardstock to fit the box or container.
2. Glue or tape corresponding images or letters back-to-back, with string or ribbon sandwiched in between. Glue beads, charms, or paper cutouts to the ribbon. Glue or tape the ribbon to the inside of the book lid.
3. Decorate the outside of the box or container as desired.

ACCORDION-FOLD GREETING (PAGE 113)

You will need:
   Resist-paper accordion card (We used a holiday design; or you can stamp plain cardstock paper with your own design, if desired.)
   Alphabet stamps
   Rubber stamps (These stamps were used for the card pictured: O094 Big Holly, T088 Poinsettia, O377 Other Big Holly, T378 Other Poinsettia.)
   (4) 2½" squares of silver cardstock paper
   (4) 2" squares of white cardstock paper
   Dye or water-based ink pads (Raised pads work best.)
   Ink brayer (optional)
   Glue

*See page 172 for materials ordering information.

1. Color each panel of the accordion card in one of 2 ways: (1) Rub the ink pad over each panel to cover with ink, and then remove the excess ink with a paper towel; or (2) Use a brayer to roll ink onto each panel to cover it.
   The pattern in the resist paper will appear because of the way it "resists" taking the ink. When working on each panel, be sure to avoid bleeding ink onto the other panels; either fold the other panels out of the way or mask them with plain paper. Color the background of the panels as desired.
2. After the background colors are dry, begin stamping, using the stamps in a random pattern on each panel. Be sure to mask the panels you are not working on to protect them from stamping.
3. Use the alphabet stamps to stamp the letters for NOEL on the 2" white cardstock squares. Center and glue 1 stamped white square to each 2½" silver square. Then center and glue the stacked squares to the panels to spell out your greeting.

Enlarge or reduce pattern on copier to desired size.

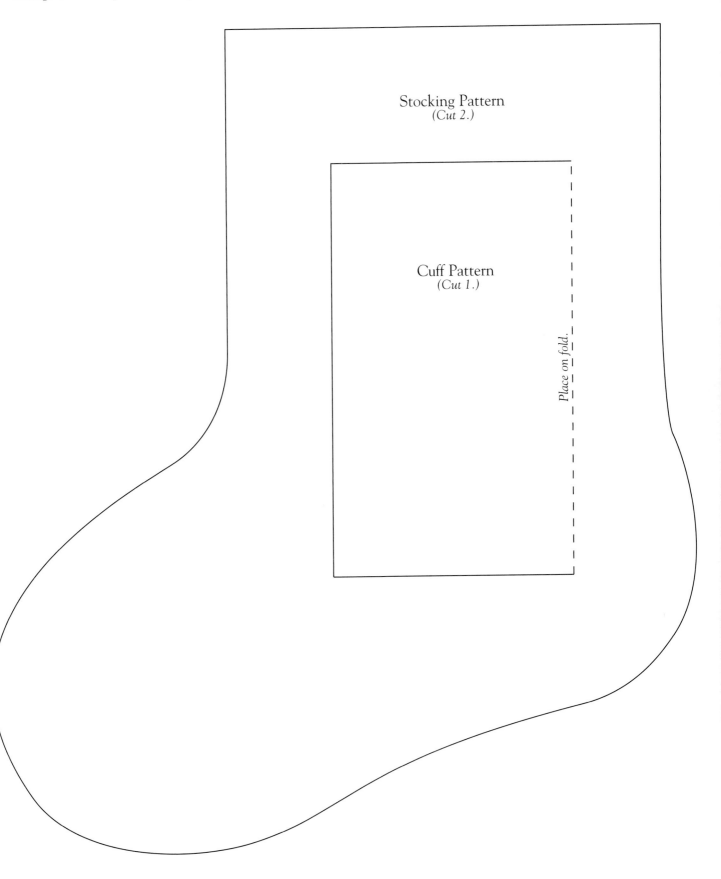

Stocking Pattern
(Cut 2.)

Cuff Pattern
(Cut 1.)

Place on fold.

A RING OF LEAVES (PAGE 64)

You will need:

Velvet (Acetate-rayon blend works best.)

Water in mister bottle

Fusible interfacing

Rubber stamps used for wreath pictured: J249 small
   open fern, F240 flower leaf, I248 Tahitian leaf, H245
   Matisse leaf, L113 grape leaf, Q326 open line oak,
   and Q324 solid oak leaf

Styrofoam wreath form

Ribbon to wrap wreath

Glue (optional)

*See page 171 for rubber stamp ordering information.

1. To imprint the velvet, place the desired rubber stamp,
rubber side up, on the ironing board. Lightly mist each
side of the velvet. Lay the velvet, right side down, on the
stamp image. Place fusible interfacing on top of the area
being pressed. (The interfacing keeps the velvet from
fraying and reinforces the leaves.)

2. Using the part of the iron that has no steam holes,
press the iron to the fabric, and count to 20; lift the iron,
being careful not to move the fabric. Press again, count to
10, and lift the iron. (If steam holes are evident on the
velvet, use a Teflon pressing cloth.)

3. Wrap the wreath form with ribbon, securing the ribbon
with straight pins. Cut out the leaves, and attach them to
the ribbon-wrapped wreath form with straight pins; reinforce with glue, if desired.

FELT-WRAPPED BOOKS (PAGES 108–109)
Snowflake Pattern

Enlarge or reduce pattern on copier to desired size.

RIBBON NAPKIN HOLDERS (PAGE 27)

For 8 napkin holders, you will need:

2 yards of 2"-wide decorative ribbon

2 yards of 2"-wide satin ribbon for the lining

8 Velcro™ dot sets

Fusible interfacing

8 buttons

Cut both ribbons into (8) 7¾" lengths. Center and sew
the hook section of a Velcro dot on the right side of 1
length of satin ribbon, 1¼" from 1 end. Center and sew
the loop section of the Velcro dot on the right side of
1 length of decorative ribbon, 1½" from 1 end.

Pin the ribbons, right sides together, with the Velcro
dots at opposite ends. Lay a piece of fusible interfacing
(cut to the same size as the ribbons) on top of the

ribbons. Sew the
ribbon ends only,
forming a V-shaped
point at the end with
the hook section of
the Velcro dot and
sewing the opposite
end straight across.
Trim excess fabric.

Turn the ribbons
right side out. Following
manufacturer's direc-
tions, fuse the ribbons together along the length of the
napkin holder. (The interfacing fuses the ribbons together,
eliminating the need for side seams.) Sew a button at the
point. Repeat to make 8 napkin holders.

Alphabet
Enlarge or reduce desired letters on copier to desired size.

A TIMELESS ARRANGEMENT (PAGES 62–63)

For the Mantel Scarf, you will need:

- 5 coordinating fabrics
- Interfacing
- Trim, jingle bells, and tassels
- Hot-glue gun and glue sticks

Note: The mantel scarf pictured is for a 60"-long mantel. To make a mantel scarf this length, enlarge the pattern pieces 50%. To custom-fit the scarf to your mantel, measure the mantel, and adjust the pocket patterns accordingly.

1. Measure the length and the width of your mantel. Add 1" to the length and 11" to the width; cut a rectangle out of fabric to this measurement.

2. Cut the following, using different fabrics as pictured:
   - 1 pocket from Pattern 5
   - 2 pockets from Pattern 4
   - 2 pockets from Pattern 3
   - 2 pockets from Pattern 2

3. Line pockets with interfacing, and stitch the pockets together in the following order, as shown on the diagram: 2, 3, 4, 5, 4, 3, and 2.

4. On the right side of the rectangle, lay the row of pockets, right side up, along 1 long edge of the rectangle. Stitch along the pockets' bottom curves and seams. Trim close to the seam along the pockets' bottom curves and sides.

5. Fold the opposite long edge of the rectangle under and stitch to hem.

6. Cut 2 pockets from Pattern 1, and then cut 2 (11" x 13") rectangles from the same fabric as the large rectangle. Line the pockets with interfacing.

7. Lay 1 pocket on each rectangle, right sides up, and stitch along the sides and bottoms. Trim close to the seam along the pockets' bottom curves and sides.

8. Sew 1 pocket section (from Steps 6 and 7) to each short edge of the large rectangle.

9. Glue decorative trim along all of the raw edges to cover.

10. Using a needle and thread, tack tassels and jingle bells to embellish the mantel scarf, as desired.

Mantel Scarf
Pocket Placement Diagram

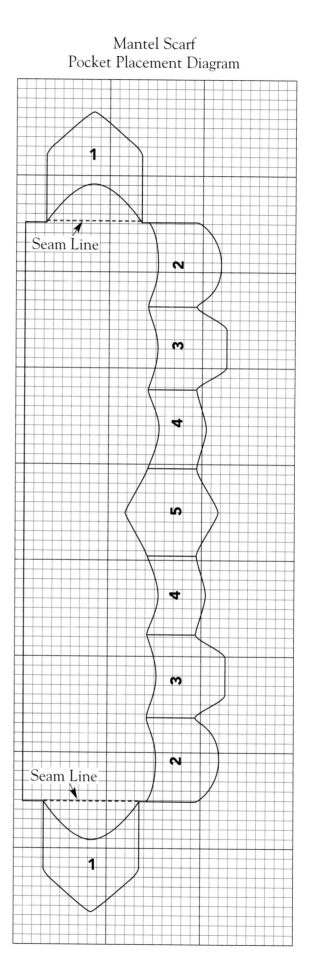

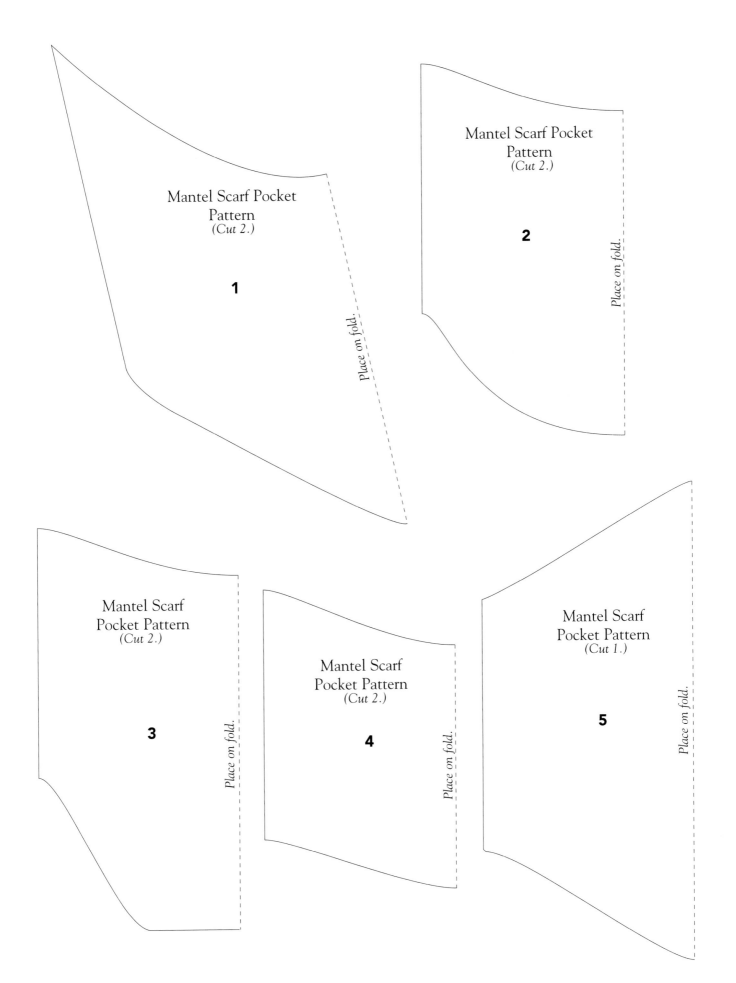

Mantel Scarf Pocket
Pattern
(Cut 2.)

1

Place on fold.

Mantel Scarf Pocket
Pattern
(Cut 2.)

2

Place on fold.

Mantel Scarf
Pocket Pattern
(Cut 2.)

3

Place on fold.

Mantel Scarf
Pocket Pattern
(Cut 2.)

4

Place on fold.

Mantel Scarf
Pocket Pattern
(Cut 1.)

5

Place on fold.

WHERE TO FIND IT

Source information is current at the time of publication.

Beads: Contact Beadbox, Inc., 1290 N. Scottsdale Rd., Suite 104, Tempe, AZ 85281; or visit www.beadbox.com.

Candles: Contact Rose Ann Hall Designs, 1413 23rd Street, Galveston, TX 77550. RAH Mexican church candles are available in 36 sizes and 6 different gift sets in fine stores across the U.S.

Candy & confections: Contact Hammond Candy Company, 4969 Colorado Blvd., Denver CO 80216; or call (303) 333-5588.

Cover—antique glass cake pedestal: Contact Christine's, 2822 Petticoat Lane, Birmingham, AL 35223.

Fresh greenery garlands & wreaths: Contact Laurel Springs Christmas Tree Farm, LLC, 7491 Hwy 18 South, Laurel Springs, NC 28644; or call (800) 851-2345.

Permanent greenery garlands & wreaths: To find the Michael's Arts and Crafts Store nearest you, call (800) 642-4235, or visit their Web site at www.michaels.com.

Styrofoam™ forms: To find the Michael's Arts and Crafts Store nearest you, call (800) 642-4235, or visit www.michaels.com.

Pages 10–11—antique glass cake pedestal: Contact Christine's, 2822 Petticoat Lane, Birmingham, AL 35223.

Pages 10–11—angel, pieplate & urn: To contact a *Southern Living* At HOME™ Consultant near you, visit www.southernlivingathome.com.

pages 10–11

pages 110–111

Page 12—antique leather chairs: Contact Bridges Antiques, 3949 Cypress Drive, Birmingham, AL 35243; or visit their Web site at www.bridgesantiques.com.

Page 12—small urn & snowball candles: To contact a *Southern Living* At HOME Consultant near you, visit www.southernlivingathome.com.

Page 12—white pots: Contact Potluck Studios, 23 Main Street, Accord, NY 12404.

Page 13—luncheon plate: To contact a *Southern Living* At HOME Consultant near you, visit www.southernlivingathome.com.

Pages 16–17—casserole dishes: Contact Williams-Sonoma, Inc., P.O. Box 7456, San Francisco, CA 94120-7456; call (800) 541-1262; or visit www.williams-sonoma.com.

Page 24—antique glass cake pedestal: Contact Christine's, 2822 Petticoat Lane, Birmingham, AL 35223.

Page 24—antique cake box: Contact Tricia's Treasures, 1433-5 Montgomery Hwy, Vestavia Hills, AL 35216; or call (205) 822-0004.

Page 24—luncheon plate: To contact a *Southern Living* At HOME Consultant near you, visit www.southernlivingathome.com.

Pages 26–27—angel, pieplate, snowball candles & urns: To contact a *Southern Living* At HOME Consultant near you, visit www.southernlivingathome.com.

Page 27—glass bowl & napkins: Contact Williams-Sonoma, Inc., P.O. Box 7456, San Francisco, CA 94120-7456; call (800) 541-1262; or visit www.williams-sonoma.com.

Pages 28–29—beaded trees: Contact Gold Leaf Designs, 337 N. Oakley Blvd., Chicago, IL 60612.

Pages 28–29—background tapestry: Contact Bridges Antiques, 3949 Cypress Drive, Birmingham, AL 35243; or visit their Web site at www.bridgesantiques.com.

Pages 28–29—glass cake pedestals: Contact Two's Company, 30 Warren Place, Mt. Vernon, NY 10550; or call (915) 664-2277.

pages 28–29

Pages 28–29—napkin rings/place cards: To contact a *Southern Living* At HOME Consultant near you, visit www.southernlivingathome.com.

Page 29—china, Hemisphere pattern: Contact Bromberg & Co., 2800 Cahaba Road, Mountain Brook, AL 35223; or visit their Web site at www.brombergs.com.

Page 33—antique glass cake pedestal: Contact Christine's, 2822 Petticoat Lane, Birmingham, AL 35223.

Page 39—red-and-white striped bowl: Contact Lamb's Ears, 3138 Cahaba Heights Road, Birmingham, AL 35243.

page 39

Page 41—table runner: Contact Lamb's Ears, 3138 Cahaba Heights Road, Birmingham, AL 35243.

Page 42—soup server: Contact Lamb's Ears, 3138 Cahaba Heights Road, Birmingham, AL 35243.

Page 44—tart server: Contact Lamb's Ears, 3138 Cahaba Heights Road, Birmingham, AL 35243.

Pages 46–47—green dinnerware: Contact Horchow, 111 Customer Way, Irving, TX 75270; or call (800) 456-7000.

Pages 46–47—red dinnerware: Contact Pier 1 Imports, 301 Commerce Street, Suite 600, Fort Worth, TX 76161; call (800) 447-4371; or visit www.pier1.com.

Pages 46–47—candles: Contact Crate & Barrel, 725 Landwehr Road, Northbrook, IL 60062; call (800) 323-5461; or visit www.crateandbarrel.com.

pages 46–47

Pages 46–47—candlesticks: Contact Two's Company, 30 Warren Place, Mt. Vernon, NY 10550; or call (915) 664-2277.

Pages 46–47—place mats: Contact Seibels, 135 West Oxmoor Road, Homewood, AL 35209.

Pages 46–47—flatware: Contact Ross-Simons, P.O. Box 20990, Cranston, RI 02920; call (800) 556-7376; or visit their Web site at www.ross-simons.com.

Page 47—red-checked buckets: Contact Charles Keath, 1265 Oakbrook Drive, Norcross, GA 30093.

page 47

Page 54—tray: Contact Seibels, 135 West Oxmoor Road, Homewood, AL 35209.

Page 54—green custard bowls: Contact Williams-Sonoma, P.O. Box 7456, San Francisco, CA 94120-7456; call (800) 541-1262; or visit www.williams-sonoma.com.

Page 55—package wrappings: Contact Loose Ends, LLC, P.O. Box 20310, Keizer, OR 97307; call (503) 390-7457; or visit www.looseends.com.

Page 57—grapevine wreaths: To find the Michael's Arts and Crafts Store nearest you, call (800) 642-4235, or visit www.michaels.com.

Page 57—red-checked buckets: Contact Charles Keath, 1265 Oakbrook Drive, Norcross, GA 30093.

Pages 57 & 60—oversize pinecones: Contact Loose Ends, LLC, P.O. Box 20310, Keizer, OR 97307; call (503) 390-7457; or visit www.looseends.com.

Pages 60–61—fresh greenery, wreaths, garlands & trees: Contact Laurel Springs Christmas Tree Farm, LLC, 7491 Hwy 18 South, Laurel Springs, NC 28644; or call (800) 851-2345.

Pages 60–61—ribbons: Contact Hannah Silk, 1529 Laurel Street, Santa Cruz, CA 95060.

Page 61—candlestands: To contact a *Southern Living* At HOME Consultant near you, visit www.southernlivingathome.com.

Page 64—stamps: Contact Hot Potatoes Fabric & Wall Stamps, 2805 Columbine Place, Nashville, TN 37204; call (615) 269-8002; or visit www.hotpotatoes.com.

Page 68—white wire tree: Contact Smith & Hawken, 117 E. Strawberry Drive, Mill Valley, CA 94941; or call (800) 776-5558.

Page 69—stamps & velvet ornament kit: Contact Hot Potatoes Fabric & Wall Stamps, 2805 Columbine Place, Nashville, TN 37204; call (615) 269-8002; or visit their Web site at www.hotpotatoes.com.

Pages 72–79—The Caroline House Holiday Tour: Contact Briarwood Presbyterian Church, 2200 Briarwood Way, Birmingham, AL 35243; call (205) 776-5347; or visit their Web site at www.briarwood.org.

page 84

Page 84—wire baskets: Contact Tricia's Treasures, 1433-5 Montgomery Hwy, Vestavia Hills, AL 35216; or call (205) 822-0004.

Pages 88–89—chairs: Contact Tricia's Treasures, 1433-5 Montgomery Hwy, Vestavia Hills, AL 35216; or call (205) 822-0004.

Pages 88–89—china: Contact Jill Rosenwald, 51 Melcher Street, Boston, MA 02210.

Pages 88–89—ribbon: Contact Midori, Inc.; 708 Sixth Avenue North, Seattle, WA 98109.

Pages 88–89—white crackle ornaments: To contact a *Southern Living* At HOME Consultant near you, visit www.southernlivingathome.com.

Page 89—white tree candles: Contact Crate & Barrel, 725 Landwehr Road, Northbrook, IL 60062; call (800) 323-5461; or visit their Web site at www.crateandbarrel.com.

Page 91—speckled baskets and enamelware buckets: Contact Compradores, Suite 197, 132 250 Shawville Blvd., Calgary, Alberta T2Y227.

Page 94—urn: Contact French Market Antiques, 204 West Coosa Street, Talladega, AL 35160.

page 96

Page 96—china: Contact B. Ware, 31265 La Baya Unit B, Westlake Village, CA 91362.

Page 97—partridge ornaments: Contact Christmas & Co., P.O. Box 130037, Birmingham, AL 35213; or call (205) 943-0020.

Page 100—pillows and throw: Contact Metropolitan Deluxe, 225 Summit Blvd. #300, Birmingham, AL 35243; or visit their Web site at www.metropolitandeluxe.com.

page 105

Pages 104–109—felt: Contact Kunin Felt, 380 Lafayette Road, P.O. Box 5000, Hampton, NH 03843-5000; or visit www.kuninfelt.com.

Pages 110–111—beads: Contact Beadbox, Inc., 1290 N. Scottsdale Road, Suite 104, Tempe, AZ 85281; or visit www.beadbox.com.

Pages 112–113—resist paper and stamps: Contact Hot Potatoes Fabric & Wall Stamps, 2805 Columbine Place, Nashville, TN 37204; call (615) 269-8002; or visit their Web site at www.hotpotatoes.com.

Pages 114 & 117—candy canes: Contact Hammond Candy Company, 4969 Colorado Blvd., Denver, CO 80216; or call (303) 333-5588.

Page 116—wire leaf garland: Contact Loose Ends, LLC, P.O. Box 20310, Keizer, OR 97307; call (503) 390-7457; or visit www.looseends.com.

Pages 118–125—cookie houses: Contact Susann Montgomery-Clark, 2501 Laredo Circle, Birmingham, AL 35226; call (205) 823-6513; or at RodsusBHAM@aol.com.

pages 118–125

Page 123—silver dragées: Contact Williams-Sonoma, P.O. Box 7456, San Francisco, CA 94120-7456; call (800) 541-1262; or visit www.williams-sonoma.com.

Page 127—china: Contact Jill Rosenwald, 51 Melcher Stree, Boston, MA 02210.

Pages 128–129—chairs and soup tureen: Contact Henhouse Antiques, 1900 Cahaba Road, Birmingham, AL 35223; or visit www.shophenhouseantiques.com.

Page 130—bowls & plates: Contact Henhouse Antiques, 1900 Cahaba Road, Birmingham, AL 35223; or visit www.shophenhouseantiques.com.

Page 134—antique spoons: Contact Birmingham Antique Mall, Inc., 2211 Magnolia Avenue, Birmingham, AL 35205.

Page 134—new spoons: Contact Gorham, 100 Lenox Drive, Lawrenceville, NJ 08648.

Page 142—plates and cup: Contact Bromberg & Co., 2800 Cahaba Road, Mountain Brook, AL 35223; or visit www.brombergs.com.

page 152

Pages 152 & 157—china: Contact Jill Rosenwald, 51 Melcher Street, Boston, MA 02210.

Page 158—teacup: Contact Artichant, 660 Madison Avenue, New York NY 10021; or visit www.barneys.com.

Page 183—candle information: Contact National Candle Association through their Web site at www.candles.org.

Page 183—holiday decorations: Contact Midwest® of Cannon Falls through their Web site at www.midwestofcannonfalls.com.

page 129

GENERAL INDEX

page 27

Recipe Index

Eggnog Pie,
page 22

CONTRIBUTORS

EDITORIAL CONTRIBUTORS
Melanie J. Clarke
Lorrie Hulston Corvin
Connie Formby
Chloë Fugate
Margot Hotchkiss
Susan Huff
Laurie Knowles
Susann Montgomery-Clark
Duffy Morrison
Mary Benagh O'Neil
Cynthia Moody Wheeler

CONTRIBUTING PHOTOGRAPHER
Keith Harrelson

THANKS TO THE FOLLOWING HOMEOWNERS
Barbara and Leon Ashford
Kay and Eddie Clarke
Peggy and Tom Dekle
Carolyn and John Hartman
Lula M. Harvey
Merle and Doug Howard
Susan and Don Huff
Lanier and Philip Ivester
Christi and Tim Kallam
Stan Nelson
Barbara and Ed Randle
Becki and Lee Weathers

THANKS TO THE FOLLOWING BUSINESSES AND ORGANIZATIONS
Beadbox, Incorporated, Tempe, AZ
Briarwood Presbyterian Church, Birmingham, AL
Cooper Nelson Properties, LLC
Kunin Felt, Hampton, NH
Midwest® of Cannon Falls, Cannon Falls, MN
National Candle Association, Washington, DC
Nelson's Interiors, Inc.

HOLIDAY PLANNING GUIDE

Embrace the season gleefully with the help of this handy guide.
You'll find spacious calendars, tidy list boxes, and useful tips—
all in one place. With this special section, you're on
your way to the most organized, most carefree Christmas ever.

November 2001

Get a jump on the December rush. List all the things you have to do (and want to do!) during this month that sets the stage for the fun holidays to come.

Sunday	Monday	Tuesday	Wednesday
4	5	6	7
11	12	13	14
18	19	20	21
25	26	27	28

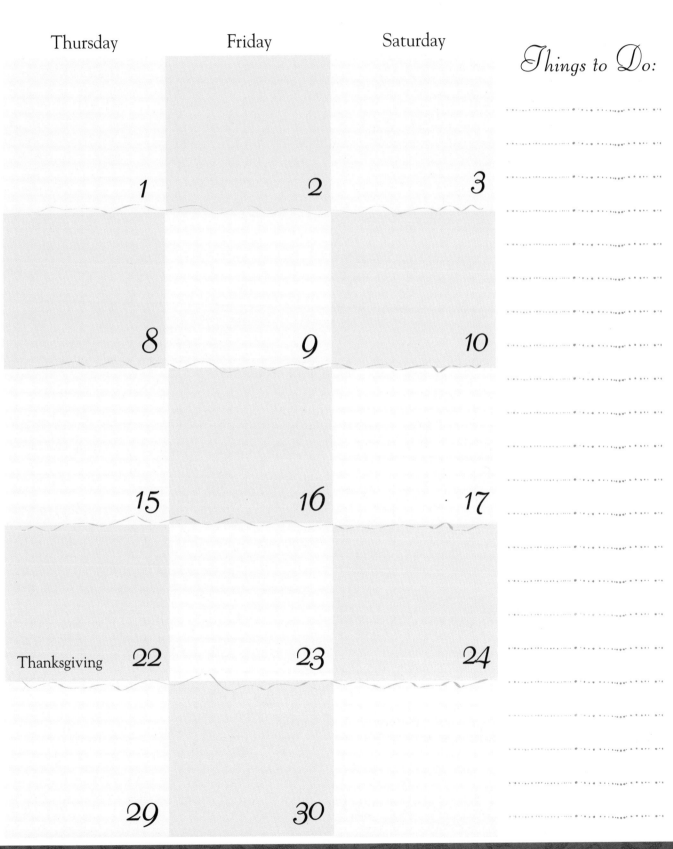

Thursday	Friday	Saturday
1	2	3
8	9	10
15	16	17
Thanksgiving 22	23	24
29	30	

Things to Do:

DECEMBER 2001

Free yourself from tiny notes scattered from the refrigerator door to the bottom of your purse. Write all of your errands on this calendar, and you'll be set for stress-free holidays.

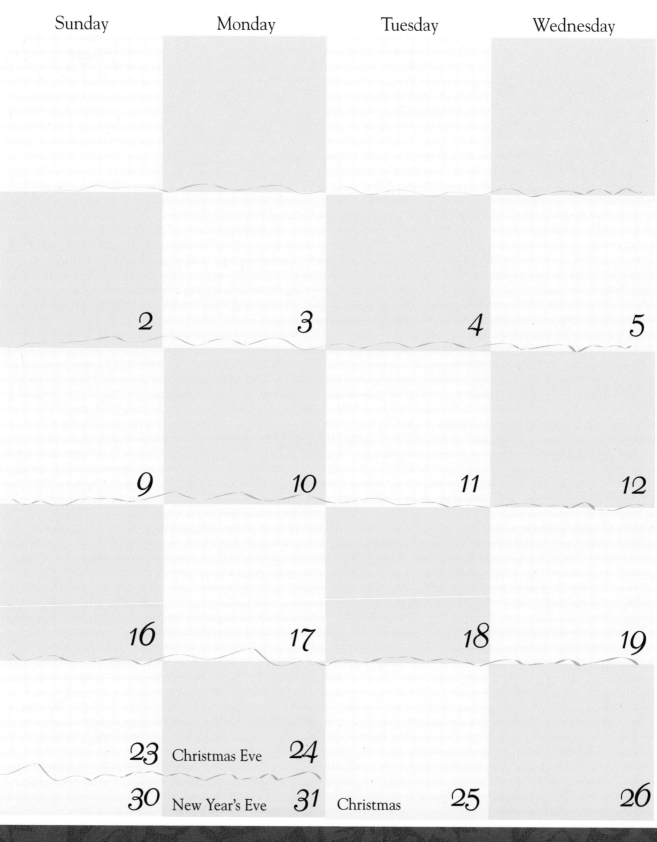

Sunday	Monday	Tuesday	Wednesday
2	3	4	5
9	10	11	12
16	17	18	19
23	Christmas Eve 24		
30	New Year's Eve 31	Christmas 25	26

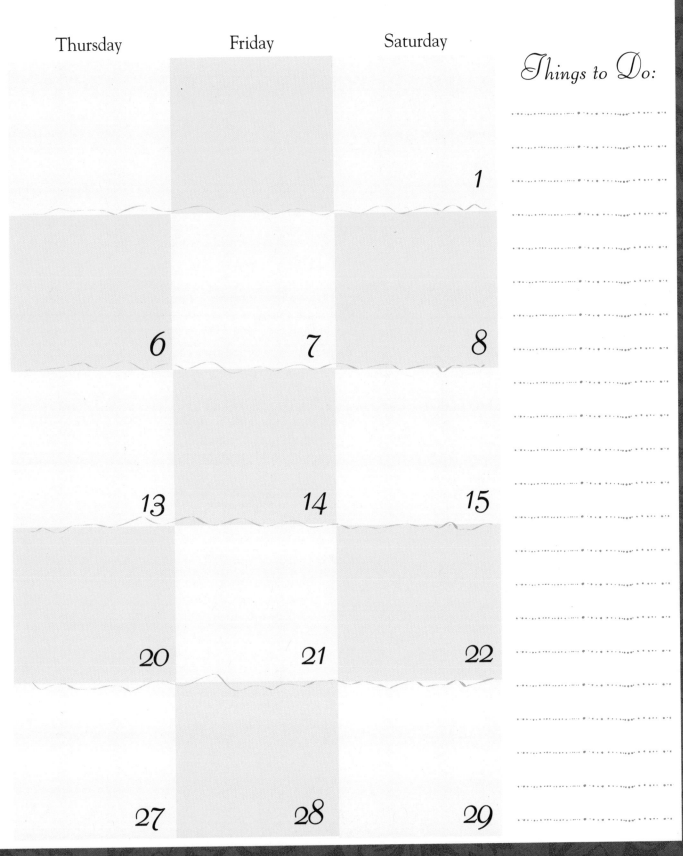

Thursday   Friday   Saturday

1

6   7   8

13   14   15

20   21   22

27   28   29

Things to Do:

HELPFUL HOLIDAY HINTS

These tips answer some of the season's basic decorating and cooking questions, leaving you more time to sit back with a warm mug of cocoa to enjoy the holidays.

Three Quick Steps to a Fancy Dessert

Most of us love to have a showy dessert to top off our Christmas menu, and while you may be short on time this holiday season, you don't have to be short on imagination. Try this idea for an easy yet impressive dessert.

1. Gather a cheesecake, a package of fancy cookies (such as cylinder-shaped or oblong, flat-bottomed Pepperidge Farm varieties), a container of ready-to-spread frosting or raspberry jam, and a satin ribbon.

2. Put the cheesecake on a pretty serving plate. Then stand the cookies on end, one by one, "gluing" them in a ring or a collar around the outside of the cheesecake with frosting or jam.

3. Tie the ribbon in a pretty bow around the cookies, and dust the top of the cheesecake with sifted powdered sugar, if desired.

Recipe Rescue

Try these quick-save cooking solutions from our test kitchens to keep you cool under the pressure of a holiday gathering.

- When a cake turns out dry or the layers fail to come out of the pans evenly, make parfaits or a trifle. Crumble the cake into glasses or a dish, and layer with whipped cream and fresh fruit.

- If your cookie dough is too dry, stir in a tablespoon or two of milk.

- If cookies harden and stick to the cookie sheet, return them to the oven for 1 minute.

- When the chocolate you are melting seizes (clumps), stir in a tablespoon of vegetable oil or shortening to smooth things out.

- To thicken a mousse, stir in whipped heavy cream.

Handy Substitutions

Find yourself without a needed ingredient for your holiday baking? Try a substitution.

- Buttermilk = 1 cup milk plus 1 tablespoon white vinegar
- 1 cup self-rising flour = 1 cup all-purpose flour plus 1 teaspoon baking powder plus ½ teaspoon salt
- 1 cup cake flour = 1 cup sifted all-purpose flour minus 2 tablespoons
- 1 cup powdered sugar = 1 cup sugar plus 1 tablespoon cornstarch. Process this in a food processor.
- 1 cup light corn syrup = 1 cup sugar plus ¼ cup water
- 1 tablespoon cornstarch = 2 tablespoons all-purpose flour
- 1 teaspoon baking powder = ¼ teaspoon baking soda plus ½ teaspoon cream of tartar

- 1 (1-ounce) chocolate square = 3 tablespoons cocoa plus 1 tablespoon butter or margarine
- ½ cup balsamic vinegar = ½ cup red wine vinegar
- 1 medium onion, chopped = 1 tablespoon onion powder
- 1 garlic clove = ⅛ teaspoon garlic powder
- 1 tablespoon chopped fresh herbs = 1 teaspoon dried herbs or ¼ teaspoon powdered herbs
- 1 teaspoon ground allspice = ½ teaspoon ground cinnamon plus ½ teaspoon ground cloves
- 1 tablespoon dried orange peel = 1½ teaspoons orange extract or 1 tablespoon grated orange rind
- 1 (1") vanilla bean = 1 teaspoon vanilla extract

Decorating with Candles

Candles add warmth, style, and mood to any setting—this seems especially true at Christmastime. Light up with decorating ideas from the National Candle Association (www.candles.org).

- Unite candles of uniform color or varying shades of one color in an assortment of shapes and widths, using a unique combination of candleholders. Such a display can look wonderful even when the candles aren't lit.

- Group different size tapers in a straight line down the center of the table, spacing them 3" apart in order of height; or put a tall candle in the center, with shorter ones going down the line on each side.

- Fill a crystal bowl with water, and add a few floating candles for a romantic centerpiece—the cut crystal will magnify the glow of the candles. When a smaller decoration is needed, put one floating candle in a wineglass filled with water.

- Make a centerpiece by placing a column candle in a pottery bowl and surrounding the base of the candle with smooth stones; or try using a porcelain bowl and faux pearls.

- Transform your fireplace into a "candleplace" by filling it with candles. Vary their heights with bricks to create the effect of a glowing flame. (This is great to do when the weather is too warm to light a fire.)

- Turn an average dinner into a celebration with candlelight, but remember it is best to use unscented candles so that only the aromas of the meal fill the air.

Candle Storage & Use

- Candles refrigerated before using will burn slowly and evenly. Wrap them in foil or plastic before refrigerating to prevent the wicks from absorbing moisture.

- Before a party, light and extinguish the candles; they'll light more quickly later.

- Votive holders will clean easily if you add ⅛" of water to each glass before inserting a candle.

Christmas Tree Decorating Tips

Ever wonder why those beautiful Christmas trees in store windows look so magical? Discover a few tricks of the trade from Midwest® of Cannon Falls to add sparkle to your tree (www.midwestofcannonfalls.com).

- Use one strand of lights per foot of tree. The lights should be strung thoughout the tree, not stretched over the tips of the branches. Tuck your lights around the trunk, weaving them in and out of the length of the branches to give the tree depth.

- Swag garland, beginning on the bottom at the back of the tree. Drape the garland from branch tip to tip, using 12" to 20" swags (depending on the width of the tree). Then twist the garland on each tip. The swags should become smaller as you go up the tree.

- Fill the spaces on the inner tree branches for an enchanting look from the inside out. Use ornaments, ribbons, garlands, fruits, toys, mirrors, small gifts, cards, or pinecones—whatever fits your theme.

- Make a strong statement by choosing a dominant subject or color for your tree. Most trees look best with decorations that balance texture, shape, size, and color; these separate elements can be tied together by making one feature dominant. For example, if your existing ornament collection has no theme, create one by introducing a significant quantity in one color or shape.

- Determine the number of ornaments you need for the size of your tree. A rough formula to follow is approximately 40 ornaments per foot of tree. To establish symmetry to your tree, hang the largest ornaments first and then the next largest and so forth. Be sure ornaments are suspended and hang freely so that they are not touching branches. Hang shiny finishes before matte or soft finishes and bright colors before muted colors. Distribute each size, shape, texture, and color over the entire tree. For a dramatic effect, cluster several ornaments, combining different colors, sizes, or shapes in one bunch; bind them together with ribbon or a bow. Place these groups symmetrically throughout the tree, or join them as a swag spiraling the tree.

ENTERTAINING PLANNER

*You entertain to have a good time and, especially during the holidays,
to create wonderful memories. Use these pages to organize
your plans for the most memorable parties of the year.*

Guest List

*List the guests you wish to invite to your holiday gathering.
Make it easy on yourself, and include phone numbers alongside the names.*

MENU

*Be sure to add a new showstopping dish to this year's
food lineup—it's a great conversation starter.*

Using Chargers

Want to try chargers, but you're unsure about their proper usage? (Chargers, or service plates, are dishes just a little bigger than dinner plates and are used decoratively under smaller plates and bowls.) You'll be relieved to know that it's perfectly okay for you to decide. Just follow these tips.

- Mix and match china and charger patterns to form interesting combinations.
- Feel free to use chargers with or without place mats or a tablecloth.
- Use gold- or silver-colored chargers with all kinds of china. Often, these can be purchased inexpensively from the housewares section of discount stores.
- Make your own chargers by spray-painting magnolia leaves or pine needle boughs in gold; then hot-glue them to cardboard cake circles.

Last-Minute Details

Get a handle on last-minute party tasks by listing them here.

Party Supplies List

From napkins to ice to flowers, you'll remember all your party supply needs when you write them down beforehand on the lines offered below.

Party To-Do List

Check guest towels, press tablecloths, light candles— it's easy to confirm all the details when you've jotted them down on a list.

CHRISTMAS DINNER PLANNER

The Christmas feast is more an event than a meal. And since every event is made easier with planning, use these pages to write down all the important details for this holiday tradition.

Guest List

Dinner To-Do List

This list can include everything from buying the food to setting the table.

MENU

Fancy Folds

It's surprising how a little creative napkin folding can go a long way in making a table setting say "special occasion."
Try one of these folds for your holiday table, and be prepared for lots of compliments on your stylish flair.

Buffet Fold

A. Lay napkin open and flat. Fold napkin in half to form rectangle, with folded edge at bottom. Fold top edge of first layer down 2" toward middle; then fold down again 2" toward bottom edge.

B. Turn napkin over. Fold right edge a third toward center. Repeat, folding this section over on itself one more time in same direction.

C. Tuck flatware into pocket.

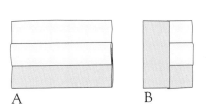

Cummerbund Fold

A. Lay napkin open and flat. Fold napkin into quarters, with closed corner pointing down toward you. Tightly roll top layer down to center.

B. Rotate napkin to right so that roll runs on a diagonal from top left to bottom right.

C. Holding roll in same position, fold left and right edges under until they meet and overlap slightly. Remaining rectangle should feature a band that runs diagonally from left to right.

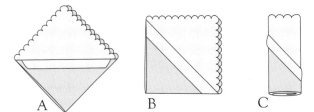

Diploma Roll

A. Lay napkin open and flat. Fold napkin in half to form rectangle, with folded edge at top. Fold top right and bottom right corners in to meet and form a triangle.

B. Roll napkin all the way up from left to right.

C. Secure napkin with ribbon or napkin ring.

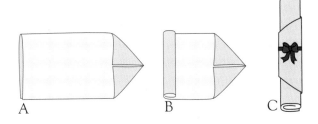

Basic Posy

A. Lay napkin open and flat. Bring lower right corner up to and beyond top edge, forming two small, equal triangles on each side.

B. Holding napkin in center of bottom edge, loosely pull napkin through napkin ring; gather in loose folds.

C. Gently shake napkin to make folds fall attractively.

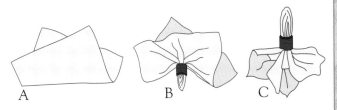

Straw Roll

A. Lay napkin open and flat, with one corner pointing down toward you.

B. Starting at bottom corner, roll napkin into a smooth tube.

C. Fold tube in half. Tie with ribbons, or tuck folded middle into goblet or glass.

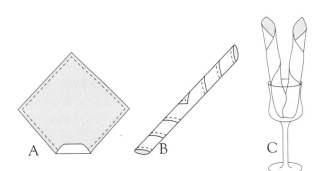

GIFTS & GREETINGS

Instead of the usual cards in envelopes and boxes tied with bows, you may be sending holiday greetings via E-mail, and your gifts may be homemade videos for family members living far away. Whichever method you choose, keep a record here for quick reference.

CHRISTMAS CARD LIST

Name	Address	Sent/Received

GIFT LIST

Name	Gift	Sent/Delivered

Care Packages

This is the time of year when good things come in all sorts of packages.
The following tips suggest ways to dress gifts in style without spending a fortune on the wrappings.

*Use a plump raffia bow to dress up gift bottles of jellies, preserves, and flavored oils and vinegars.

*Wire-edged ribbon, sometimes called French ribbon, makes tying beautiful bows easy. It's available at many discount stores, as well as floral supply and crafts stores. Purchasing one type of ribbon by the roll rather than several different ribbons by the yard saves money.

*Another budget-friendly idea is to wrap boxes in brown kraft paper, tissue paper, or even construction paper for small gifts. White butcher or packing paper also works well. Transform the paper from plain to pretty using felt-tip pens or rubber stamps.

HOLIDAY MEMORIES

Every holiday season offers its own blend of funny moments, poignant remembrances, and Christmas wishes come true. Be sure you remember every one by writing them on these pages.

Treasured Traditions

What's the first thing you think of when you think of Christmas? Chances are it's a time-honored family tradition. Record your favorite ones here, and maybe include some new ones for next year.

Special Holiday Events

Whether it's a production of The Nutcracker, *a neighborhood caroling party, or simply a gathering with close friends, Yuletide happenings provide some of the best memories of the year.*

Holiday Visits & Visitors

*There are some friends you seem to see only at Christmas. Take a moment to record the latest tidbits
about their growing families and accomplishments that you learn at these annual get-togethers.*

FAVORITE
HOLIDAY RECIPES

NOTES & IDEAS FOR NEXT YEAR

Things We Loved

List below the things that worked so well this
Christmas that they must be repeated next year.

Works in Progress

Here's the place to write ideas for parties, decorations, and recipes that you'd like to try for future holidays.

Party Ideas

Decorations

Recipes

New Year's Resolutions